Intercessors
God's End-Time
Vanguard

Intercessors
God's End-Time Vanguard

SUSAN GADDIS

Pathway
PRESS

Dedication

To the past and
present members
of my church family at
Atascadero Foursquare Church

(Malachi 3:16, 17).

Contents

Foreword

A few years ago I had the opportunity to drive up the coast of Southern California to do a story on the Diablo Canyon Nuclear Power Station. No, I was not writing about the dangers of a nuclear plant next door. This story was about the witness of several members of our denomination—highly skilled men—who were dedicated to see that more than 2 million homes across 14 states of Western America received power for living and received it safely. Because of these "custodians of power," today millions of us enjoy light, heat and other benefits of 20th-century living. Through their testimony, they had also turned the Devil's (Diablo) Canyon into a "Sanctuary of Spirit."

During this visit, I met Tom and Susan Gaddis, pastors of these custodians at the Foursquare church in Atascadero, located 200 miles north of Los Angeles. Since that time, our friendship has grown, as has the flock which Tom and Sue shepard.

In the same way one ministers out of "being," an author writes from a heart of who she is. I have found Susan Gaddis radical in her approach to intercessory prayer. Before jumping to conclusions that this is something extreme or weird, remember that the term radical actually refers to a "stem growing from the root of a plant." In linguistics, radicals are used to identify sources or relationships. In nuclear terminology, radical is the grouping of atoms together to bring fourth various kinds of reactions.

Susan Gaddis is radical in her commitment to Jesus Christ. Whether enjoying the worship of the congregation, being spoiled by the hospitality of the Gaddis home, or putting Chicken Chow Mien "into the ministry" at the local Chinese restaurant, one theme always surfaces—the magnificence and majesty of our Savior. Every part of her life is an extension of the Branch that grows out of the root of Jesse.

Susan is radical in her commitment to the Gaddis household. Who would even dare to try to write a book with six kids in the house? Add to that the demands of a pastor's wife and her involvement in standing for righteousness in many sectors of the community. She is one of the few persons I know who can stretch 24 hours into what seems like 30 or more! And yet, she finds time to be the loving wife and mom in a home that "has it together."

Above all, Susan Gaddis has discovered the secret of grouping the spiritual atoms of powerful prayer and intercession together to make a difference in our world and, in particular, in the church. *Intercessors: God's*

End-Time Vanguard is not a book filled with theory. It is a manual of experience—learned by persistence, practice and patience. And once again, we who call upon the name of the Lord must return to the reality that far too often, as love has become the lost heart of the church, intercessory prayer has become the lost art in the believer's life. Susan calls us back to the basics of intercession. She then enthusiastically suggest that we join her in the pursuit.

I encourage you to read on. You will find that the finely-tuned groupings of spiritual atoms taught in this book bring powerful results. You might also become a "custodian of power."

—Ron Williams
Communications Officer
International Church of the Foursquare Gospel

In Appreciation . . .

In writing this book, I am deeply indebted to the following individuals:

- My husband, Tom, who has endured great competition from my computer and encouraged me to "have a life beyond that of wife and mother."

- My six children, David, Mary, Katie, Jonathan, Daniel and James, who left me alone for hours at a time to think and write in quiet.

- My intercession team, Vicki, Christy, Marcie, Ronda, Sheri, Robin and Francie, who critiqued each chapter of the manuscript and walked with me in uncharted Spirit places.

- My mentor Ron Williams, who continues to encourage me as I develop my writing skills.

- My dad, Andy David, who helped me purchase a computer so I could fulfill a dream.

Introduction

abriel surveyed the map in front of him. Night was beginning to spread blackness over the Western Hemisphere. He watched the darkness quickly dim as the fire of God began to light up the spirit realm over each city and town. Gabriel enjoyed this ongoing display as each region on the map entered the night hours. Numerous homes in northern Florida lit up as people responded to his invisible messengers nudging them awake with new prayer assignments. The middle states and Canada quickly followed with their illumination of prayer. It was never really "night-dark" on this map; only "spirit-dark" in places still closed to the gospel. Even those sections were beginning to glow as intercessors countered the work of the dark spirits.

Gabriel glanced at Michael, because they were both due in the throne room. The archangel was studying the vibrating map intently. Neither of them had seen this much prayer activity since the Moravians had begun their chain of intercession years ago. That prayer meeting had lasted over 100 years and thrust missionaries into a world asleep to the Great Commission. Although briefed to expect this concentrated prayer at the end of the 20th century, they were both still surprised at its intensity. It was needed. They had work to do.

Gabriel knew Michael's troops stood equipped, as did his, for their latest assignment. Already the courtyard was resounding with talk of the King's preparations for battle. A lot depended on the intercessors below, and he hoped they knew how important their prayers were in the plans and purposes of the Father. The "end" of the end times was upon them, and the King's intercessors needed to be well prepared for the task ahead. Their participation in the unseen realm was vital to the salvation of nations and the ushering in, once again, of the King to Planet Earth.

This book is written for those who feel the call of God upon their lives to pray. Its purpose is to instruct and release intercessors to enter the fullness of their calling and to encourage those who are currently on the front lines of intercession. The foundation is Scripture and the application is practical. With these things in place, it is hoped that no reader will feel "weird" about intercession and the spirit realm. With feet firmly planted in Scripture, intercessors can be secure in their duties and experience. They will need that security to operate as part of the vanguard of God's end-time purposes, because in these last days, intercessors are on the cutting edge of God's plans.

Part I

The Person of Intercession

Chapter 1 One

The Adventure of Intercession

The current call of God upon the church includes the call to prayer. All over the world, this call is going forth as never before in history. Prayer marches are parading down city streets. Prayer teams are quietly infiltrating foreign countries to intercede for the nations, and teens are gathering around flagpoles at their schools. Churches are incorporating prayer walks into their weekly activities, and parachurch organizations are springing up to function solely for the purpose of prayer. Race and color are blended together as citizens of the kingdom of God congregate to pray for a lost and dying world. Many sense a transition taking place as we near the completion of the Great Commission. There is a common feeling of the possibility of the soon return of Jesus Christ, and numerous people believe that we are on the brink of a worldwide revival.

Some are already beginning to experience the initial signs of revival. The promise of Acts 2:17, 18 is being fulfilled before their eyes:

> In the last days, God says, I will pour out my Spirit on all people. Your sons and daughters will prophesy, your young men will see visions, your old men will dream dreams. Even on my servants, both men and women, I will pour out my Spirit in those days, and they will prophesy.

No longer does the Book of Revelation seem mysterious to many who are learning that God often speaks in symbols, pictures and prophecies. They, too, see things happening in the once unseen realm and are able to enter that activity through the doorway of prayer. These people are not willing to ignore the summons of God, which is to stand before Him and plead for the nations, because these people are *intercessors*.

Intercessors are a key factor in God's plans for the future. They are the advance team of Christians who dare to enter enemy territory through prayer and lay claim to spiritual ground held captive by the adversary of mankind's souls. Spiritual roadblocks that have hindered evangelism are being removed because of these dedicated people who take the job of prayer seriously. Their heart is for individuals and for nations. Through their intercession, the highways are cleared for the evangelists, missionaries and pastors who follow with the message of Jesus Christ. Like John the Baptist their heart's cry is as . . .

A voice of one calling: "In the desert prepare the way for the Lord; make straight in the wilderness a highway for our God. Every valley shall be raised up, every mountain and hill made low; the rough ground shall become level, the rugged places a plain. And the glory of the Lord will be revealed, and all mankind together will see it" (Isaiah 40:3-5).

What Is an Intercessor?

An intercessor is an advocate, one who represents or pleads the cause of another. Scripture tells us that both the Holy Spirit and the Son, Jesus, are intercessors for us. They petition the Father on our behalf so that His life and will may be accomplished in and through us. Clearly, some things cannot be achieved in our lives without the entreaties of Jesus and the Holy Spirit. Their compassion, love and commitment are evidenced in their continued intercession on our behalf.

In Romans 8:26, 27 and 34, we see the intercession of the Holy Spirit ministering within us, while Jesus intercedes for us as He stands with the Father:

In the same way, the Spirit helps us in our weakness. We do not know what we ought to pray for, but the Spirit himself intercedes for us with groans that words cannot express. And he who searches our hearts knows the mind of the Spirit, because the Spirit intercedes for the saints in accordance with God's will. . . . Christ Jesus, who died—more than that, who was raised to life—is at the right hand of God and is also interceding for us.

An intercessor stands before God for a lost person or for an unholy situation to request God's intervention and the working out of His will. Intercessors face the forces of darkness to enforce the victory of Calvary in what is called spiritual warfare. Intercession is listed in 1 Timothy 2:1-4 as one of several activities done on behalf of others, along with requests, prayers and thanksgiving. The activity of intercession will also incorporate these different types of prayer, as all kinds of prayer are at the disposal of an advocate as he pleads for another before the throne (see Ephesians 6:18).

In addition, an intercessor will often use a variety of spiritual gifts, such as prophecy, word of knowledge, or discerning of spirits. The Holy Spirit provides these gifts to help the intercessor achieve what God has declared must happen in the unseen realm before His will can be completed in the visible realm. These gifts frequently flow together during intercession, creating a seamless garment of praise and prayer.

Intercession is a spiritual duty all Christians are asked to share. Although many consider intercession to be one of the gifts of the Spirit, it is not a spiritual gift in the sense that some have it and others don't. We can never use the excuse, "I don't have to pray for others because I don't have the gift of intercession." The act of intercession is one of our nonnegotiable responsibilities as Christians.

Many times the spirit of intercession will fall upon

those involved in prayer, and they will find themselves praying with unusual anointing. At this point, the *gift* of intercession has empowered the *duty* of intercession. This makes the duty of intercession an exciting adventure. On the other hand, the lack of this gift doesn't negate our duty to intercede.

For some, intercession also becomes a calling to take on the *ministry* of intercession. They find great fulfillment in extended periods of prayer, often praying for several hours or more each day. They also appreciate the behind-the-scenes involvement of intercession, where they can operate in anonymity within the body of Christ, yet be a patron before the throne of God. Their spiritual sensors usually pick up on things that others have not discerned. In these last days, more and more people are being called to this frontline ministry. Much of their work is individual, but many are involved with other intercessors meeting in teams and gathering for corporate intercession.

THREE ARENAS OF INTERCESSION

There are three basic divisions of intercession: individual intercession, team intercession, and corporate intercession. Most intercessors operate in at least two of these arenas; many find themselves involved in all three.

1. *Individual intercession.* This arena of intercession is private, involving only ourselves and God in the seclusion of our prayer life. This is where most of us begin learning intercession. Our concern for hurting family or friends drives us to our knees, where we desperately cry out for God's intervention. Few will pray for our children with the intensity that we will. Few will pray for

our mate or parents with the same fervor as we, because they do not feel the depth of love we hold for those close to us. Love motivates us to contend in prayer for the well-being of our family, and it is in the "doing" that we begin to learn the skills of intercession. Eventually, we expand our prayer focus to include additional prayer assignments given us by the Holy Spirit.

Individual intercession might be compared to the commando who carries out warfare duties. Working alone, he is able to infiltrate and wreak havoc inside enemy territory. Ezekiel 22:30 records that only one man was needed to stand in the gap on behalf of the nation of Israel. All that was needed at that point in time was *one*.

Moses stood alone before the Lord and pleaded for his people (see Psalm 106:23). It was a young David who stood alone before a mighty Goliath and fought for a nation (1 Samuel 17); and it was a lone woman named Jael who took a tent peg in her hand and drove it through the head of the sleeping Sisera, securing freedom once more for Israel (Judges 4).

2. Team Intercession. Some battles require a larger military unit. This second category is where prayer groups form at any time and for any purpose. Often it is just a onetime event as when the pastor asks the congregation to turn and gather in groups of three or four to pray for specific needs. But when a group continues to meet over a period of time, it becomes a *prayer team*.

A prayer team involves two to as many as 12 people, who gather regularly for prayer. We might compare this category of intercession to a commando unit: an elite group of soldiers who train together and operate in synchronization with each other on the battlefield. Each member knows the strengths and weaknesses of every member of the unit and adapts accordingly. Together they form a troop that can invade and secure larger areas of enemy territory.

Team intercession will supply support and strength not found in individual intercession. Deuteronomy 32:30 affirms that one may chase a thousand, but two are able to put ten thousand to flight. Ecclesiastes 4:12 further states, "Though one may be overpowered, *two* can defend themselves. A cord of *three* strands is not quickly broken."

In 1 Samuel 14, we find the story of Jonathan, King Saul's son, and his armor-bearer confronting a Philistine detachment. Only King Saul and Jonathan had weapons, because the Philistines had forbidden the making of arms. Israel was outnumbered and without armament. Jonathan and his armor-bearer slipped away from the main forces and approached the Philistine outpost. Seeing only two men coming against them, the Philistines began to jeer. Jonathan took the taunting of the enemy as a sign from the Lord to attack and boldly climbed the cliff separating the Philistine camp from the Israelites. Within minutes, 20 men were killed. The ground began to shake and a God-intended panic swept over the entire Philistine army. Confounded by a fleeing enemy, Saul's forces quickly pulled themselves together and pursued the Philistines. All the Lord needed were *two* to initiate a mighty victory.

3. *Corporate Intercession.* The word *corporate* carries the idea of unity and legality within a body of people. When we assemble each week on Sunday mornings, we

convene as a local expression of the corporate church headed by Jesus Christ. We meet as one body of people operating under the appointed leadership of a pastor and elders. The corporate church is likewise represented in the assembling of a March for Jesus or a denominational convention. Any large gathering of believers who assemble under designated leadership can be a representation of the corporate church. They denote a united body taking legal action in the unseen realm for the kingdom of God through worship, teaching, prayer, or the administration of Kingdom sacraments and business.

Corporate intercession takes place whenever Christians gather as a united body under delegated leadership to pray for a specific purpose. Usually this takes place within a local church service. But it may also happen in a larger arena. Intercessors who assemble for the March for Jesus or the Meet You at the Pole gatherings of young people are functioning as corporate intercessors. Pastors who come together to intercede for their community carry great authority in the spirit realm because they constitute legal spiritual jurisdiction in their community. We are currently beginning to see national and international gatherings for corporate intercession take place through leaders such as C. Peter Wagner, John Dawson and Cindy Jacobs. Corporate intercession might be compared to a large-scale military invasion by the forces of God against the forces of darkness.

The most well-known example of corporate intercession is recorded in the first two chapters of the Book of Acts. Jesus had left the disciples with instructions to wait in Jerusalem to receive power before they began to carry out the Great Commission. A total of 120 people—including the disciples, some women, the mother of Jesus and His brothers—met in an upper room for prayer. Kingdom business was conducted during that prayer meeting by seeking the Lord for a replacement for Judas in the leadership of the group. Undoubtedly they also prayed for the promise of power that Jesus had told them was essential for the advancement of the gospel. It came—suddenly! The outpouring of power that resulted from that time of corporate intercession changed their lives, produced 3,000 new believers and established the church! (see Acts 1:12—2:41).

Understanding the differences in these types of intercession is important because an intercessor will operate differently within each category. Individual intercession provides great freedom and abandonment between the individual and the Holy Spirit. Many expressions of intercession acceptable in private times of prayer might be inappropriate and cause distraction in corporate intercession. Alone, the agenda for intercession is developed as one senses the leading of the Holy Spirit and moves accordingly.

Team intercession involves praying with others, learning to synchronize our "giftings" with theirs, and working through the little personality conflicts that usually arise within a team. It's a great opportunity for further development as an intercessor. We'll be affirmed, stretched and challenged in ways seldom imagined. The Holy Spirit's agenda for team intercession usually unfolds as the team works together. No longer will we get the whole picture for the time of intercession, but the mind of the

Lord will be discovered as the team interacts with one another and the Holy Spirit.

Corporate intercession requires more restrictions on an intercessor, because we must function under the leadership of the assembly and adjust our personal intercession style to the style of the group. Our prayer agenda is determined by those in authority as they listen and receive direction from the Holy Spirit. The power that comes from corporate intercession depends upon submission to those in leadership and willingness to operate as part of a whole.

Application

1. We are living in a time of renewed interest in the activity of intercession as many realize the important role of prayer in these latter days. What evidence have you seen or heard that would indicate an increase in the activity of intercession on a national and international level? Why are you personally interested in reading a book about intercession? What do you hope to gain from your study?

2. Intercessors are praying as individuals, in teams, and gathering for corporate intercession while the Holy Spirit globally interweaves their efforts into His overall purposes. What experience have you had in each of these categories?

3. Why might team intercession be more challenging

for a person than individual or corporate intercession?

4. What might be some ways that the members of a team could learn each others' gifts and synchronize their strengths and weaknesses?

The Marks of an Intercessor

"*N*ow I lay me down to sleep. I pray the Lord my soul to keep. God bless Mommy and Daddy, Amen." Every child who knows this prayer has begun the adventure of intercession. A child's prayers are as much regarded in the courts of heaven as an adult's. The words may be simple but they give security to a child who needs the peace of Jesus to enfold them in pleasant dreams.

Scripture places no great qualifications upon an intercessor. All believers have a duty to pray for others and especially for those in authority (1 Timothy 2:1-4). All that is required for someone to pray is a growing relationship with Jesus and a willingness to walk in obedience to His directions. Yet, in over 20 years of ministry and involvement in individual, team and corporate intercession, I have observed certain distinguishing marks that accompany those who are serious about a ministry of intercession.

Satan will try to defeat us at the basic points in which he fell: pride, rebellion against authority, and division among the followers of the Most High. We counter these attempts by being people of godly character, in particular, intercessors who are humble in the practical application of their calling.

CLEAR-MINDED AND SELF-CONTROLLED

Self-control and clear thinking keep pride at a distance, because it is within our emotions and minds where pride subtly gains a foothold. Once that foothold is established, prayer becomes clouded. In Peter's first letter to the early church, he makes an interesting statement: "The end of all things is near. Therefore be clear minded and self-controlled so that you can pray" (1 Peter 4:7). Considering that we are reading this nearly 2,000 years later indicates that we must be near the "end of the end" of all things! Peter admonishes us to be clear-minded and self-controlled for the expressed purpose of praying competently. In other words, end-time intercessors must take their duties seriously and not allow any substance or wrong reasoning to influence them. Nor should they easily lose control of their tempers, emotions or desires.

Believers struggling with drugs or alcohol shouldn't consider a *ministry* of intercession until they are free of these controlling influences. Often people may not know just how much these substances can cloud their ability to hear the voice of the Lord. Their own need should draw them to others for prayer and accountability, but they should not be released into ministry for individual or team intercession until such controlling elements are conquered.

Wrong reasoning can also cloud our ability to think clearly. Knowing the Word and its principles are vital to an intercessor. Misconceptions and wrong reasoning stem from a lack of scriptural understanding. Intercessors must learn to filter their opinions and thought processes through a grid of truth based on Scripture. Intercessors will tune into their *self-talk* and evaluate it against the Word of God. If their reasoning fails to align with Scripture, then they will change directions. Team intercession is a wonderful place to learn this, if the members are willing to dialogue about their thought life and hold each other accountable.

Two of my closest friends, who have been involved with me in intercession and leadership continue to hold me accountable for clear-mindedness. Christy tends to cut to the heart of the matter: "You're wrong. You can't think like that. Scripture says . . ." Bev uses a more gentle approach, usually asking lots of questions to readjust my perspective: "Why are you thinking that? Do you think that is Scriptural? Perhaps you might want to approach it from another angle. Do you remember the verse that says . . .?" This works both ways. I also reserve the right to hold them accountable in their thought life. Together we make a great team!

In his letter, Peter also links self-control with one's

ability to pray effectively. Emotions and desires should never be a controlling element in an intercessor's life because they can be a hindrance to prayer. We need to maintain dominion over these areas and not allow them to govern us. This doesn't mean that we won't express strong feelings; only that the feelings will operate under the rulership of the Holy Spirit.

I am a redhead (sprinkled with gray). For years, I felt free to blame my bursts of temper on my hair color. I also have six children and have sometimes used my mother-hood exhaustion as an excuse for irritability. Then there were those occasional "problem people" within the congregation my husband pastors who could be blamed for my moodiness. One day, however, a friend pointed out how quickly my temper or moodiness came under control when I answered the phone. "Grumble, grumble, snap, snap" became a sweet-sounding "Hello, this is the Gaddis residence. May I help you?" It didn't take long to realize *what* was controlling *whom*! I began to exercise more discipline over my emotions around the house by using a controlled tone of voice when speaking with my family. I soon proved the "red hair" theory wrong and found that self-control was possible. An added advantage of my newfound self-control was an increased effectiveness in intercession. The apostle was right!

RIGHT RELATIONSHIPS

The last place we want Satan to gain an advantage over us is in intercession, yet we are vulnerable in this area because we relate with folks in need, with other intercessors, and with leaders. In 2 Corinthians 2:11,

Paul admonishes us to be knowledgeable, not ignorant, of the Enemy's devices. Verse 10 identifies one of these devices as unforgiveness. More intercessors are sabotaged by the Enemy's darts of offense and unforgiveness than in any other area.

Life is filled with opportunities to be mistreated, misunderstood, rejected and misrepresented. Jesus encountered all of these; should we expect less? My husband has often said that ministry would be wonderful if it wasn't for the people! But people are our assignment and they often hurt us. Far more dangerous than the injuries caused by other people is the unforgiveness we carry inside. Wounds that become infected with unforgiveness are impossible to heal apart from radical spiritual surgery. Untreated they become roots of bitterness which trouble us, and eventually defile others (see Hebrews 12:15). When we choose to forgive those who have hurt us, we shut the door in the face of a greater Enemy who seeks to gain leverage in our lives.

Sandy had been deeply hurt by abuse and rejection from her parents and others. Unspeakable things had been inflicted upon her, which resulted in sleepless nights, tormented thoughts, and an inability to trust. Her husband and young son were feeling the repercussions of her agony. As a Christian, Sandy had tried to close the door to the Enemy's intrusions by going through the motions of forgiveness. But the anguish continued.

One day, as she was receiving prayer, Jesus asked Sandy to relinquish all those instances of injustice to Him. Sandy panicked. These things had become her identity. Each time Jesus would begin to extract them, Sandy would reach up and pull them back. "No!" she cried. "These things are mine! I've paid for them with my blood and they are mine."

"No, Sandy," Jesus firmly replied. "These things are Mine! I bought them with My blood and I have come to claim them."

That day Sandy found freedom from the torment of the Enemy because she was finally able to release to Jesus what was rightfully His. Forgiveness is more than simply saying, "I forgive you." It is giving to Jesus that for which He suffered and died. Our sorrows, pains and iniquities were all placed upon Him so we might have peace (see Isaiah 53:4, 5). We no longer retain lawful claim to offenses, whether they are our own or another's, because ownership of sin and wounds belong to Jesus.

Sometimes we are the cause of hurt, intended or not. Consequently, many of us may find it easier to forgive others than to say, "I was wrong. Please forgive me." Occasionally the strain in a relationship isn't easily traced to a single individual. But it still needs to be addressed. This doesn't necessarily mean that the problem will be resolved, only that we are willing to move in reconciliation. We are only accountable for our attitudes and actions. How another responds is not our responsibility. Even if the reaction is unfavorable, at least we have fulfilled our obligation as a believer to seek restoration of the relationship. If the response is gracious and forgiving, then reconciliation is realized. Scriptural reconciliation consists of an attitude of love and forgiveness between two parties, even though they continue to hold differing opinions.

There are times when we need to extend forgiveness to another without involving that person, because the offense is one-sided and exists only from our perspective. The other party may be unaware of any hurt we have received. I remember the confusion and hurt I felt when a friend walked up to me and said, "I forgive you for not doing a good job as a pastor's wife, and I ask your forgiveness for gossiping about you to other members in the church."

I was shocked! As a young pastor's wife I knew I wasn't doing things the way my predecessor had, but I had no idea my friend had been offended by my immaturity. I was certainly surprised to find that my lack of experience had been a topic of conversation among those whom I was trying to serve. Her offense was one-sided, and forgiveness should have been sought before the throne and from those in whom she had confided. Her repentance before God and before those she had involved would have allowed her to extend patience and graciousness to me. Speaking of it to me only complicated the problem by involving me in something about which I had no knowledge.

Identifying our hurts and where the responsibility for them lies is the beginning of right relationships. We need to spend time with the Lord in relinquishing our ownership of personal sin, injuries or pain. Only then are we ready to move in reconciliation with others. Knowing we need to forgive an offender or seek another's forgiveness is one thing; walking it out is another. Head knowledge must become footwork to an intercessor.

"Therefore, if you are offering your gift at the altar and there remember that your brother has something against you, leave your gift there in front of the altar. First go and be reconciled to your brother; then come and offer your gift" (Matthew 5:23, 24).

UNDERSTANDING SPIRITUAL AUTHORITY AND SUBMISSION

We all have arenas of influence and leadership. It may be our home, our community, our place of employment or within our church. We also have others to whom we are accountable. Whenever we interact with people, we must conduct ourselves with the grace and wisdom of the Lord Jesus Christ, whom we represent to those we lead and those who direct us. Our attitudes and actions concerning our own authority and those over us have direct bearing on our influence in the spirit realm.

Spiritual warfare requires an understanding of our authority in Christ Jesus, and how to operate under the authorities He has placed in our lives. The hosts of hell respect authority and respond to those who bear the name of Jesus. They also know if a person is in rebellion to God-appointed authority. They view such a person as one like themselves, for they invented rebellion. It is only through submitting to authority that one can move effectively in delegated authority against the rank and file of the Enemy host.

In his Gospel, Matthew relates an incident that happened in Capernaum (8:5-13). A centurion approached Jesus concerning a paralyzed servant. The day had been full of teaching and ministering to folks, but Jesus took the time to stop and listen to this Italian who represented the oppression of Rome. The story touched Jesus, and He offered to go and heal the servant. The centurion explained that the visit would be unnecessary—all that was needed was a word from Jesus for the servant to be cured. He explained that, as a centurion, he operated under authority, with soldiers under him who obeyed his word. He knew how authority operated. He knew that whatever was causing his servant's illness would have to obey any word Jesus spoke. This explanation astonished Jesus, and He commended the faith of this man above all in Israel (8:5-10).

Intercessors are like that centurion. They will walk into any situation and ask, "Who's in authority here? Who's in charge?" Once they have that information they adjust themselves to working under that person (or persons). Submitting under another does not always mean agreeing with every decision made. We may not like their style of leadership, or we may feel they do not display the maturity needed for their position. It doesn't matter. I'm sure the centurion found himself in that type of situation many times. At some point during his army career he had probably suffered under unreasonable authority. Yet, he aligned himself and governed those under his command. His understanding of spiritual authority was tied into his understanding of submission, which directly affected his faith. It was this faith that astonished Jesus and resulted in the healing of the servant.

Growing up, my mother would have me make lunch for the family. She gave a few general directions and then left the rest to my own creativity. "There's tuna in the pantry and peanut butter in the cabinet. There might be some leftover roast in the refrigerator too." Lunch time could be quite elaborate and was often spread all over the kitchen.

My dad, on the other hand, was more direct. He would instruct me to make grilled cheese sandwiches, fried in butter, and grilled for only two minutes on each side. At any time during the lunch process, he would feel free to adjust my way of cooking or serving those cheese sandwiches. Dad's style of leadership was different from Mom's. His way was confining, but it taught me to be an efficient cook! How I prepared lunch depended on who was at home and, therefore, my authority for that day. It was my responsibility to discover who was in charge and adjust accordingly.

Different people, churches, Christian organizations and denominations hold varying philosophies of church government. The denomination I belong to operates from a modified hierarchical view of church government. Essentially, that means that authority rests with the appointed leadership. Pastors are appointed to churches by the denominational authorities. The direction and plans of a local church are decided by leaders whom the pastor designates. A friend attends a church that is congregational in their view of church government, which means authority rests with the congregation. Pastors are hired and fired by the congregation, and direction and plans are decided by leadership that the congregation has elected.

Sometimes, people who transfer to a new church don't realize that the government of the new fellowship may be different from what they have experienced in the past. The leadership style of the pastor and others may also be different. This can lead to misunderstandings and open a door to the Enemy for offense and division among God's people. To avoid this, intercessors should find out the governmental philosophy of their church and learn the leadership styles of those they serve.

People in leadership often expect us to automatically understand these things about authority and submission, even when we don't! Therefore it is up to us to cultivate an attitude of godly submission that is reflected in our actions. Once we have demonstrated a submitted heart in our relationship with an authority, we usually find that we have gained the right to discuss decisions and optional ways of doing things. Most leaders want to hear different perspectives on plans and decisions, but they need to know that we are all headed in the same direction.

Our adversaries watch with interest to see if we grasp this principle of spiritual warfare. The implications of mishandling authority can be disastrous (see Romans 13:1, 2). Many intercessors sabotage their prayers because this requirement has been neglected. Therefore, great intercessors know how to move in authority, how to be great followers, and how to be examples of submission to those observing (Titus 3:1, 2).

SPIRITUAL "GIFTINGS" DO NOT EQUAL MATURITY OR AUTHORITY

The Greek word *charisma* is often translated as the "operational power of God." It originates from the word *charis*, which means "grace." *Charisma* can also be defined as "God's grace extended in unearned and unconditional outpourings of God's power." We call these "gifts of the Holy Spirit." They are free, outward displays of God's grace, initiated by the Holy Spirit.

Spiritual gifts are like tools in an intercessor's hand. Our prayer time becomes more focused as we operate in words of knowledge, prophecy, discerning of spirits, and the other gifts listed in 1 Corinthians 12:7-11. The Holy Spirit will often incorporate His gifts into a time of intercession, so that those praying know exactly what is going on in the unseen realm and what to do about it. To an intercessor, it is like receiving top secret information direct from headquarters concerning a mission assignment. However, because these gifts are outside our natural abilities and accomplish great results, they often draw attention to the one who operates in them. There is the tendency to look upon that person as one who has a mature walk with God. After all, don't wonderful things happen? They must really have a close relationship with the Lord!

One young pastor made the mistake of placing a very gifted, but immature, prophet in charge of an intercession team. Before too long, the new leader had assumed a role of authority greater than that of the pastor, because those involved did not understand that his prophetic gift was not a qualification for leadership. Many young intercessors have looked to be mentored by those moving strongly in spiritual "giftings," without researching that mentor's level of maturity and wisdom. Imbalance has resulted.

Scriptural qualifications for leadership are always based on maturity in the Lord, not on spiritual giftings. In 1 Timothy 3:1-13, there is a list of requirements for those placed in positions of authority. Each condition mentioned for leadership focuses on godly character as a sign of maturity rather than on giftings. Some ministries, such as evangelist or prophet, may indicate one's placement within the body of Christ, but it is godly character that qualifies that person to move from trainee to leader.

Over and over, I have run into damaged intercession teams who made the mistake of equating spiritual giftings with maturity. Gifts are given to young and old, experienced and inexperienced, wise and foolish alike *without qualification*—that is why they are called "free." God gives these gifts knowing that they may be misused by the immature or rebellious. Yet He doesn't require that they be returned. In other words, God does not *loan* out His gifts; He *gives* them to be freely used in ministry to others.

In contrast, godly character is not free. There is no magic wand the Holy Spirit waves over us to declare us "gifted with maturity." Christian maturity is developed over years of hammering out the principles of Scripture in our walk with God and in our relationships with people. Of course we'll make mistakes, and sometimes fall on our faces. But we must get up and try again. Eventually we'll realize that we really are making progress. But it takes time! Spiritual gifts are *free* without qualification, whereas spiritual maturity and godly character are *earned* over years of obedience. As we grow in godly character, we are able to move responsibly in the giftings God gives us.

In 1 Corinthians 14:26-33, Paul teaches us that it is possible for the gifts of the Holy Spirit to be misused. They need to be evaluated by others for the benefit of all. Neither the gift nor the person ministering the gift is cast aside, but accountability and training are necessary. Teachableness and practice will always be essential if we are to become proficient with our giftings.

Intercessors are not required to have great maturity, nor even possess a gift of the Spirit, but we dare not look to someone as a spiritual mentor or as a qualified leader based only on their ability to prophesy or give a word of knowledge.

INTERCESSORS KEEP CONFIDENCES

Many times intercessors will be asked to pray about deeply personal matters. This requires that the intercessor be someone who can be trusted with private information. Nothing will ruin an intercessor's reputation quicker then sharing knowledge that is confidential (see Proverbs 11:13). Qualified intercessors are well known for their ability to keep secrets, not for their available knowledge of other people's business. Besides knowing how to keep people's secrets, an intercessor also knows how to keep God's secrets.

One day Jesus took His three closest disciples—Peter, James and John—up onto a mountain, where He was transfigured before them. It was an awesome experience. Not only was Jesus transformed into breathtaking radiance, but Moses and Elijah appeared and the voice of Father God spoke directly to the three disciples. Now this could really get people's attention! But on the way down the mountain, Jesus instructed them to not tell anyone what they had seen until after He had been raised from the dead (see Matthew 17:1-9). Why would Jesus ask that they not speak of something that would bring glory to God? The Lord has a purpose and a season for everything; sometimes we are allowed to participate in those plans and other times not. The three disciples were allowed to observe the transfiguration of Jesus, but they didn't understand its purpose. Therefore, they were asked to keep quiet about it until after the Resurrection, when they would have the full picture of God's plan of redemption. God sees the whole picture, while we see only snapshots.

Mary, the mother of Jesus, was another who was a participant in God's plans, but she chose to treasure her experience in her heart and ponder its meaning (Luke 2:19). Intercessors are often asked to pray about things of which they are given partial knowledge. This is good for us, as it keeps us from becoming too prideful about our part in the purposes of God. Other times we will be shown things that are wonderful and exciting as God uses us to bring heaven's plans into earth's reality. But again, we may often find that He will not allow us to share those experiences with others.

Not everyone will understand the things we experience in intercession. Sharing those experiences may bring confusion or cause misunderstanding. This doesn't mean an intercessor is more privileged than another; it simply confirms the personal and individual aspect of prayer. What may make perfect sense to one person may puzzle another.

Not being allowed to speak of the things God shows us in prayer can be a real pride-killer. This isn't to suggest that we won't *ever* share our intercession experiences. Many times we can and should share those things that would encourage and strengthen others. But our sharing will always be with permission from the Lord and others involved. Periodically, we will share the things we've seen with those who need to know about them in a timely manner. Whether in prayer or conversation, it is vitally important for an intercessor to act responsibly with confidential information.

1. Prayer, for the Christian, is something that requires only a heart needing to connect with God. However, those desiring to become serious intercessors should consider the five additional qualifications discussed in this chapter. Do you agree? Explain.

2. Each of the distinguishing marks discussed in this chapter are designed to work against the growth of pride, rebellion and discord in the ministry of an intercessor. Can you recall a time when Satan was able to defeat an intercessor or group of intercessors because one of these five marks was neglected? If yes, describe the situation in your own words.

3. The five distinguishing marks discussed in this chapter are important points of accountability for an intercessor whether praying individually, on a team or involved in corporate intercession. Use the following checklist to see if you meet the qualifications of a committed intercessor:

Am I free from the influence of drugs or alcohol?

- Am I clear-minded—willing to let others challenge my reasoning and thought processes?

- Have I been exercising discipline over areas in my life that have often lacked self-control?

- Is there anyone with whom I need to make things right before I go to prayer?

- Am I willing to submit to the authorities involved in this time of intercession? Can I "switch gears" if they indicate I need to do so?

- Do I clearly understand that having spiritual giftings do not validate maturity in the Lord?

- Am I willing to have my spiritual gifts evaluated by others?

- Am I willing to keep confidential those things shared during intercession, unless released to do so by those in authority, those regarded in prayer and others who are praying with me?

Chapter 3 Three

The Internal Design of an Intercessor

*G*iving the wheel of the car another kick, I turned and headed toward a pay phone. Hopefully, my husband could look into the inner parts of this contraption and figure out how to get it going again. The car and I were not communicating well. I turned the ignition key and it growled back at me. My intention of getting from the grocery store to home did not seem important to my car. It had its own agenda for the day, and I did not know how to get it to adjust to mine! If only I understood all those hoses and greasy things under the hood, then maybe I could restore the working relationship between my car and me!

Intercession is often like the relationship I had with my car. Sometimes we know we need to pray, but we have trouble understanding our inner "sensings" and how they interrelate to the spirit world and the physical world. An intercessor wants to be able to function in both worlds comfortably.

Understanding Our Spirit, Soul and Body Design

In trying to explain the makeup of men and women, many theologians attempt to identify three aspects of human experience. The first (the spirit) is that which relates directly to God and interrelates with the spiritual dimension such as angels, dreams and the supernatural. The second (the soul) is the internal part of a person, which includes the intellect, emotions and choice. The third aspect is the human body, through which the first two aspects evidence themselves in practical, daily living. In 1 Thessalonians 5:23, we find a reference to these three parts of a person: "May God himself, the God of peace, sanctify you through and through. May your whole spirit, soul and body be kept blameless at the coming of our Lord Jesus Christ."

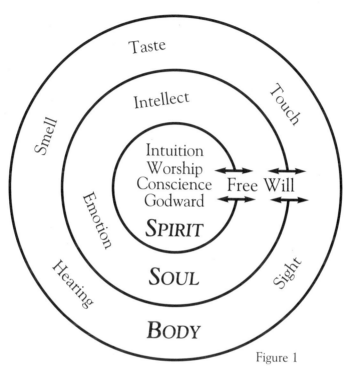

Figure 1

When God created Adam in the Garden of Eden, He first built a body out of the elements of the earth. This body was able to communicate with the physical world through the five senses: touch, sight, hearing, smell and taste. God also created this man with a soul that possessed emotion, intellect and a free will. He then *breathed* His own life into that body, giving Adam a spirit. The word *spirit* means "breath" and is that part of humans that allows them to communicate with God through intuition, conscience and worship.

Adam and Eve functioned as complete human beings, interacting with the physical world and with God. Their spirits could freely communicate with God, who is Spirit, while their physical bodies tended the garden and ruled over its creatures. The spirits of these first humans also provided a place for God's grace, love and fellowship to reside. Intuition, conscience and a desire to worship were all placed within their spirit. It was the core of their being, the place where their sense of "I" originated. They were designed for fellowship—a house for the Spirit of God. Together, the Holy Spirit and a person's spirit would rule over the soul and body, thereby enabling the person to be all that God intended.

Having a soul helped Adam and Eve process the things of their spirits into the physical aspects of life. God gave Adam and Eve intelligence. They could think, reason, understand and possess knowledge. They also felt and expressed emotions. The additional gift of free will allowed them to make choices. Possessing a soul allowed them to convey the things of the spirit into physical expressions such as obedience, praise, communication, gentleness, self-control and the other aspects of the fruit of the Spirit contained in Galatians 5:22, 23. We might say that their soul was the translator between their spirit and body.

The bodies designed for Adam and Eve were probably beyond anything we can imagine, because they were untouched by sin and decay. These bodies allowed the couple to operate in a physical world called earth and provided a means to physically express the things of their soul and spirit. Physical love, laughter and reproduction were possible because of a body. Communication of thoughts, ideas, and the decisions of Adam and Eve depended on a body. Even the work of tending the garden would have been impossible without a physical body.

THE CONSEQUENCES OF ADAM'S SIN

All this changed with Adam's disobedience. The use of his free will in deciding to disobey God cost Adam and Eve at all three levels of their existence: spirit, soul and body. Sin invaded their lives, and a holy God would not dwell with sin. The life of God, which had resided at the core of their being, vacated their spirit and Adam and Eve felt disconnected from God. Death immediately took hold and they became dead *toward* the Lord.

Not only was their spirit deadened, but their soul felt the effects of sin. Overwhelmed with guilt, Adam and Eve hid themselves from God. Their thoughts became confused with a desire to justify and defend themselves before God. No longer was there the living Spirit of God within humankind to help rule over their thoughts, emotions, and decisions, or over their body.

Seeing their spiritual and physical nakedness, God sacrificed an animal, using its skin to clothe Adam and Eve and its blood to spiritually cover their sin. Expelled from the garden, Adam and Eve left with a decaying body to house their dying souls and deadened spirits. Many years later, their bodies were destroyed by physical death.

For thousands of years this was the condition of people: their spirits dead toward God; their souls unable to correctly function as God intended; and their bodies that eventually lived for a period of 60 to 80 years. Although the spirit was deadened toward God, it was not dead toward other spirits. People began to fill their empty innerperson with the worship of other gods. At the same time, their soul level became increasingly fleshly, governed by desires, thoughts and decisions that reflected their self-centeredness. Disease and decay began to eat away at Adam's descendants. Instead of being ruled by the Spirit of God, they now became ruled by the sin that had taken God's place (see Romans 5:12).

They were unable to bring the Spirit of God back within their spirit, because sin was a part of their makeup, their lineage and their heritage. No longer did they possess the nature of God, but they possessed a sinful nature. People reflected the sin Adam chose over the God he rejected. The best that could be done was a yearly sacrifice that provided a blood covering to hide sin from God. No permanent eraser was available . . . until Jesus came.

THE NEW BIRTH

Jesus walked upon earth as the sinless God-man. Sin was not in His bloodline, because His lineage was of Father God. When His sinless blood was shed upon the cross as payment for Adam's and all of humankind's sin, it provided a new nature for those who would choose God and reject sin. We know this as repentance (see Romans 5:17-19). It was only after the Cross that people were again able to receive the Spirit of God into their spirit, replacing the old nature of sin. Following His resurrection, God once again breathed upon people the breath of life: "Again Jesus said, 'Peace be with you! As the Father has sent me, I am sending you.' And with that he breathed on them and said, 'Receive the Holy Spirit'" (John 20:21, 22).

The disciples, who stood before Jesus and received the same breath of life that had been breathed upon Adam, were the first to experience what is called the *new birth*.

Their deadened spirits became alive toward God as the Holy Spirit came to live within. Worship, intuition and conscience were again in godly operation as people were able to communicate "spirit to Spirit" with God. Salvation had come to humankind at the deepest level of their existence (Ephesians 2:4-9). This new birth is still happening today with those who repent of their sins and believe on the Lord Jesus Christ as their Savior (Romans 10:9).

Unfortunately, at the new birth, the soul of new Christians is not changed as totally as their spirit. Their soul is in the process of being restored or saved. You know this is true by looking at your own thought life. Is it always thinking pure and kind thoughts, or do you sometimes get critical and think on things you know are wrong? How about your emotions? Ever lose your temper or want to throw a giant pity party and invite the whole neighborhood? Then there's that free will that is a part of your soul. Does it ever get you into trouble by choosing unrighteous thoughts and emotions?

You get the picture: you've got a new, clean, righteous spirit that has a soul that isn't totally changed yet. But it will be, for it is in a process:

> Praise be to the God and Father of our Lord Jesus Christ! In his great mercy he has given us new birth into a living hope through the resurrection of Jesus Christ from the dead, and into an inheritance that can never perish, spoil or fade—kept in heaven for you, who through faith are shielded by God's power until the coming of the salvation that is ready to be revealed in the last time. . . . For you

are receiving the goal of your faith, the salvation of
your souls (1 Peter 1:3-5, 9).

Note the present tense in this passage indicating a
process, not a once-and-for-all event.

What about our bodies? Did they experience salvation? All it takes is one look to know the answer to that
question! Our bodies are still in the process of decay and
will not experience redemption until Jesus returns and
gives us new, incorruptible bodies. "Not only so, but we
ourselves, who have the firstfruits of the Spirit, groan
inwardly as we wait eagerly for our adoption as sons, *the
redemption of our bodies*" (Romans 8:23, italics added). In
a letter to the church at Corinth, Paul further stated:

> I declare to you, brothers, that flesh and blood can-
> not inherit the kingdom of God, nor does the per-
> ishable inherit the imperishable. Listen, I tell you a
> mystery: We will not all sleep, but we will all be
> changed—in a flash, in the twinkling of an eye, at
> the last trumpet. For the trumpet will sound, the
> dead will be raised imperishable, and we will be
> changed (1 Corinthians 15:50-52).

Note the future tense in these verses indicating that a
new body will be given to us sometime in the future.

It is the spirit part of man that is re-created and
becomes totally new at salvation (see 2 Corinthians
5:17). That salvation which happened at our spirit level
must now be worked out into our soul level.

> Therefore, my dear friends, as you have always
> obeyed . . . continue to work out your salvation
> with fear and trembling, for it is God who works
> in you to will and to act according to his good
> purpose (Philippians 2:12, 13).

With your cooperation, God begins to work *out* of you what He put *in* you! Working out your salvation takes time, and the process isn't always pleasant! Emotions can become quite intense and self-focused and strongly self-willed. Having opinions, strong emotions and a strong will are not necessarily bad. It is damaging only when they are centered on *self*. These areas of the soul slowly change as we learn to allow God's Spirit to rule.

You have probably noticed changes in your thinking patterns, emotions and will. Old fears are gone and your responses are more godly. The selfish dictates of the soul must be replaced by the spiritual dictates of the new spirit in communion with the Holy Spirit (John 3:6). This process is called Sanctification, and occurs as you hear the truth of God's Word and obey the Holy Spirit (17:17).

This is important for an intercessor to understand, because it is at the spirit level that most communication with God takes place. God is Spirit and He wants to fellowship with us at that level. This communication is then processed through the soul level of a Christian in order to be expressed by the physical body in prayer, praise or to other people:

> For who among men knows the thoughts of a man
> except the man's spirit within him? In the same way

no one knows the thoughts of God except the Spirit of God. We have not received the spirit of the world but the Spirit who is from God, that we may understand what God has freely given us. This is what we speak, not in words taught us by human wisdom but in words taught by the Spirit, expressing spiritual truths in spiritual words. The man without the Spirit does not accept the things that come from the Spirit of God, for they are foolishness to him, and he cannot understand them, because they are spiritually discerned (1 Corinthians 2:11-14).

Looking again at Figure 1, you will notice that the *will* of man is open to both our spirit and our body. Our will is the doorway between our spirit, soul and body. It gives each of us the ability to shut God off or to open ourselves up to listen to Him. It is the key to putting our decisions into action. For example, I can choose to ignore the voice of the Spirit when He warns me that my irritable disposition is out of line with my new nature. Or, I can choose to obey the Spirit's voice and change the direction my thoughts and emotions are going. I can express or repress the fruit of the Spirit to those around me. As an intercessor, I can choose to obey the Spirit's nudge to pray, or I can choose to watch TV instead. How I respond with my will to the prompting of the Holy Spirit determines the degree of sanctification in my life. The gift of free will is one of the greatest gifts given to mankind and sets him apart from the rest of creation.

The human race is unique in its privilege to experience the new birth and its consequences. Jesus said, "I tell you the truth, no one can enter the kingdom of God unless he is born of water and the Spirit. Flesh gives birth to flesh, but the Spirit gives birth to spirit" (John 3:5, 6). Each of us has passed from a mother's womb where our infant bodies developed within a sack of water. It was that physical birth which produced our fleshly bodies. Only the Holy Spirit can give spiritual birth, and He does so solely to those who have had a physical birth and believed on the Lord Jesus Christ. In other words, this new birth, or salvation, is not available to any other being, angelic or demonic; only those of Adam's race. It is this new race of beings, made up of a spirit alive with God's Spirit, who are the citizens of the kingdom of God.

Intercessors need to understand their spiritual design as eternal, spirit people who live in a body and possess a soul. Functioning as spirit people should not be uncomfortable or unfamiliar, for intercession involves spiritual things in the unseen realm. Intercession originates from our spirit and is communicated by our soul and body. It is as the Holy Spirit communes with our spirit that we begin to understand with our intellect. Job 32:8 states it well: "It is the spirit in a man, the breath of the Almighty, that gives him understanding."

ANOINTED INTERCESSION

The Holy Spirit is also *with* us. Before His death, Jesus promised the disciples, "The world cannot accept him [the Spirit of truth], because it neither sees him nor knows him. But you know him, for he lives *with* you and will be *in* you" (John 14:17). The Holy Spirit walked with people throughout the Old Testament and until Jesus finished His work of redemption. Then the promise Jesus gave in John 14:17 was fulfilled in the same manner as in 20:21, 22. He who walks with us also lives within us. He continues to walk with those who have not experienced salvation, always seeking to draw them to the love of the Father through the work of the Son.

But there is another dimension of the Holy Spirit's activity with believers. He comes *upon* the person in whom He already dwells. In Acts 1:8, Jesus said, "But you will receive power when the Holy Spirit comes *on* you; and you will be my witnesses in Jerusalem, and in all Judea and Samaria, and to the ends of the earth." Acts 2:2-4 records the first incident of the Holy Spirit coming *upon* new Christians with fire and the power that was imparted to them as a result: "Suddenly a sound like the blowing of a violent wind came from heaven and filled the whole house where they were sitting. They saw what seemed to be tongues of fire that separated and came to rest *on* each of them. All of them were filled with the Holy Spirit and began to speak in other tongues as the Spirit enabled them."

This outpouring of the Holy Spirit *upon* believers happened after the Holy Spirit had already come to live *within* them. This was a separate event, where they were *filled with the Holy Spirit*. We call this experience the baptism with the Holy Spirit, for it fulfills John the Baptist's prophecy of Jesus in Matthew 3:11: "I baptize you with water for repentance. But after me will come one who is more powerful than I, whose sandals I am not fit to carry. He will baptize you with the Holy Spirit and with fire."

This description of being filled with the Holy Spirit also matches Jesus' prophecy from John 7:37-39:

> On the last and greatest day of the Feast, Jesus stood and said in a loud voice, 'If anyone is thirsty, let him come to me and drink. Whoever believes in me, as the Scripture has said, streams of living water will flow from within him.' By this he meant the Spirit, whom those who believed in him were later to receive. Up to that time the Spirit had not been given, since Jesus had not yet been glorified.

When we are baptized with the Holy Spirit, rivers of living water overflow from deep within, gushing out through the soul and body in a supernatural experience.

Later, in Acts 2:38, 39, Peter stated that the baptism with the Holy Spirit is for all Christians throughout all ages. Neither is this baptism a onetime immersion, for Ephesians 5:18 admonishes us to be filled with the Holy Spirit. The Greek tense for *filled* in this verse indicates a continuous action; it is to be an ongoing event for the Christian.

Powerful times of intercession happen when the Holy Spirit, who is *in* you, also stands *with* you and rests *upon* you. The expression of this will vary from person to person and from situation to situation, because the Holy Spirit is ever original in working with each individual's personality. Intercession can be intense, sweet, sudden or measured and it takes on different styles and forms with different people.

1. The trinity of a person was explained in this chapter as spirit, soul and body. What part of this description has challenged the way you view yourself? How might this teaching help you to view others differently?

2. Describe some specific areas of change that you have seen in your own soul (mind, emotions and will) since becoming a Christian.

3. What did the author mean by the *will* being a doorway in your soul? How have you used this *doorway* in obeying or ignoring the prompting of the Holy Spirit?

4. Using your own words, explain the author's description of anointed intercession. Do you agree with this explanation?

How an Intercessor Hears the Voice of God

I'd had it! I called Mary and Kay and asked them to meet me at the church for a concentrated time of intercession. Things had gotten too far out of hand, and it was time to take action. Several people had left the church citing differences of opinion with the church leadership. We thought it had been a clean departure and we had given our blessing to the move. Later we found that criticism and discord were still being sown in our fellowship by those who had left. Although we spoke to those involved, our spiritual antennas were still picking up signals of strife.

This particular morning, I had been awakened early by the Holy Spirit and reminded that we weren't dealing with people, but with a critical spirit that was seeking to undermine the work of God. I could feel its tentacles of criticism reaching out to entrap unsuspecting members in the congregation. I knew these people—they were godly friends who sincerely wanted to walk in righteousness. They knew the danger of criticism. I also knew that the enemy of our soul has ways of infiltrating people's reasoning through hurts and misunderstandings. We needed to move from the place of talking with people to dealing with the spirit that was behind their actions.

As Kay, Mary and I prayed, a picture began to unfold in my mind's eye. I saw the three of us dressed in white robes, holding large swords. Before us lay a meadow of green grass with an army tank parked in the middle. The grass surrounding the tank had turned brown as if it had been sprayed with weed killer. I sensed that this tank represented the critical spirit seeking to roll over the people in the church. As I began to describe the scene, scriptures came to mind, so I spoke them aloud. As I spoke, the tank began to fall apart and soon lay in a heap upon the ground. Suddenly, birds flew over our heads and began picking up pieces of the tank and carrying them into the distance. Green grass and wild flowers immediately sprang up in its place.

The interesting thing about this time of intercession was that while I was seeing all this and speaking forth the things I felt the Holy Spirit wanted me to pray, Kay and Mary were receiving additional information from the Holy Spirit. One of them literally smelled a horrible stench as the tank was demolished. She later detected the sweet fragrance of wild flowers as they grew where the tank had been. The other heard all the sounds associated with what I was seeing. She heard the roar of the tank's engines and the clanging as it fell apart. She heard the birds flying over our heads and felt the wind caused by their wings brushing against her face.

Does this sound weird? Unconventional as it may sound, it worked! The criticism stopped. This didn't mean we never had to face the foe of a critical spirit again; but, for this time and place, it was finished. The different ways each member of the team heard from the Lord allowed us to synchronize in accomplishing God's objectives. Learning to hear the voice of God takes practice; it helps to understand how He speaks to us.

When you live with someone for a long time, you know their response to many of the things you say. If the person is critical, the response will be negative. But if the person is jovial, the response may be lighthearted. As you begin to really know a person's character, you can almost anticipate what the comments will be in dialogue. This same principle works with God. The more we know of His character and His ways, the more clearly we hear His Spirit speak to us. We know what to expect. We expect to find His character confirmed in the things He tells us.

We all experience times when we are angry with or complaining about another person. Immediately we feel a grating in our spirit and an almost audible voice telling us, "Knock it off! Change your attitude!" Hopefully our reply is, "Yes, Lord," because His character does not support a negative, complaining heart.

YOUR SPIRITUAL ANTENNA

In 1 John 2:20, 27, we read where each of us has received a permanent anointing or unction from God that will teach us the things we need to know as believers. This anointing is a form of *knowing*, even before our intellect fully grasps the information. It is that godly intuition that resides within our spirit and lets us know if something is off-base or right on target. Intercessors call this their spiritual antennas.

You may have experienced your spiritual antenna working when your teenager seemed to be doing fine but, deep inside, you knew something was wrong. Further probing revealed that your "gut feeling," or spiritual antenna, was in fact picking up something you needed to know. Perhaps you have awakened in the middle of the night sensing that a friend immediately needed prayer, only to find out later that the friend had narrowly escaped a dangerous situation. Occasionally, you might have sensed a heaviness within that felt like depression. Further investigation revealed that God was actually calling you to pray for someone who was seriously ill or experiencing a major problem.

The intuition that resides within your spirit is able to pick up on all sorts of things that your mind may not immediately comprehend. Have you ever listened to someone teach on the radio or TV and felt "warning signals" that caused you to search your Bible to see if the teacher was doctrinally unsound? You probably found your concerns justified. The "warning signal" was sensed before knowledge or understanding occurred.

The Holy Spirit also uses this spiritual antenna to warn you when an unholy spirit is in the vicinity. We may sense an inner alarm, signaling that something unclean is near. This discerning of spirits always ignites at the level of our inner spirit, which is very uncomfortable with anything unclean. This then translates into understanding or knowledge within our soul.

DREAMS AND VISIONS

Dreams and visions are other examples of how God interacts with our spirit and then filters the information through our soul. In his book *Preaching and Teaching With Imagination*, Warren W. Wiersbe says: "We think in pictures even though we speak and write with words." Perhaps that is why God chose the Hebrew people as the means to bring His message of salvation to mankind. Their culture and language are filled with pictures, vivid symbols, emotion and imagery.

Even Jesus taught with stories that formed pictures in peoples' minds and provided a wonderful means of remembering His teachings. Today God still uses imagery to communicate from the spirit to the soul. Wiersbe emphasizes the importance of imagery by quoting Horace Bushnell, "God gave man imagination that He might have a door to enter by." God births something within our spirit and then filters it up through our soul in the form of a picture in our imagination.

Sometimes, a picture comes to our mind during the night in a supernatural dream totally outside of our conscious thinking processes. Other times we may have a vision in our mind's eye, like the one I described during intercession at the beginning of this chapter. Some visions are more in the realm of reality and actually appear to be happening, as was the case in Daniel's vision recorded in Daniel 10.

Walking by the riverbank, Daniel met an angelic being. This messenger from heaven had come to give Daniel important information. The incident caused Daniel to feel weak and overwhelmed. The angel touched Daniel to give him strength and then delivered his message. What

Daniel saw, heard and felt was very real; but only Daniel saw the angel. The other men with Daniel felt terror at something they could not explain or see, so they fled. This experience was not a dream or a vision in the mind of Daniel—it was an actual physical encounter.

God often stirs our spirit as a call to prayer and then places a symbol or simple picture in our minds to help us see and sense what He wants us to pray. He frequently uses metaphors and similes. Some even see words before their eyes, as on a billboard or a ticker tape, that help them understand the direction to go in prayer. These all can happen within a dream, a vision in your mind's eye or in the physical realm of reality.

HEARING

Besides seeing, intercessors may also hear things! Remember my friend who heard the sounds of the things happening in my vision? Others have heard God speak to them within their mind. Some have heard God's voice in an audible experience. This was the case with young Samuel, who heard God call him by name in the middle of the night. He mistakenly thought it was the voice of Eli the priest! Isaiah 30:21 says, "Whether you turn to the right or to the left, your *ears* will hear a voice behind you, saying, 'This is the way; walk in it.'" Audibly hearing the Holy Spirit's voice is rare; not the normal way we hear from God.

Usually communication from the Holy Spirit takes the form of intuition or pictures translating into our understanding, and some may hear God's voice speaking in their head. Acts 10:9-22 records Peter's experience with both a vision and hearing the voice of the Holy Spirit. Whether this was in his head or out loud, we don't know, but Scripture says, "While Peter was still thinking about the vision, the Spirit said to him, 'Simon, three men are looking for you. So get up and go downstairs. Do not hesitate to go with them, for I have sent them'" (vv. 19, 20).

SONGS AND SCRIPTURE

Another way of hearing the voice of the Spirit is through a song or scripture. Have you ever awakened in the morning with a Scripture chorus running through your mind? Oftentimes you won't even be conscious of it until you find yourself singing in the shower or during the drive to work. Usually, you will find that the words to the song are things the Holy Spirit is wanting you to know.

Other times a Scripture verse will suddenly pop into your mind, and you can be assured that it is the Holy Spirit drawing your attention to something. His mission within is to teach and remind us of all the things Jesus wants us to know. "The Counselor, the Holy Spirit, whom the Father will send in my name, will teach you all things and will remind you of everything I have said to you" (John 14:26). This is one reason it is so important to memorize and meditate on God's Word—it gives the Holy Spirit tools to communicate with us.

THE PEACE OF GOD

Experiencing the peace of God is another way God communicates with us. Paul talks about the peace of God mounting guard or acting as a sentry over our hearts and minds after a time of prayer:

> Do not be anxious about anything, but in every-
> thing, by prayer and petition, with thanksgiving,
> present your requests to God. And the peace of
> God, which transcends all understanding, will
> guard your hearts and your minds in Christ Jesus
> (Philippians 4:6, 7).

An inner sense of peace is how many intercessors
know when they have finished praying about a situation.
It is God's way of saying, "Good job, you're done for
now." This supernatural peace settles over their spirit
and soul and acts as a guard against further anxiety.

I have also talked to many intercessors who use this
sentry of peace as a gauge for knowing the urgency of a
prayer assignment. They will raise their spiritual antenna
and, if they sense a peace about the problem, they will
still pray. But if they sense turmoil, they know the problem needs more serious prayer.

THE SENSE OF SMELL AND PHYSICAL FEELING

There are other ways that the soul and body interacts
with the spirit, such as the ability to physically smell things
in the spirit realm or even physically feel things. Remember
the encounter between Daniel and the angel? Daniel felt
the angel touch him and impart strength to his body. In the
Book of Revelation, John saw, heard and felt the things happening in the vision that he was told to record. These were
very real events happening to him: spirit, soul and body. He
even experienced the taste of sweetness when the angel
gave him a little scroll to eat; but once he had eaten it, the
small scroll turned sour in John's stomach. The experience

had spiritual significance for what he was commanded to prophesy (Revelation 10:9-11).

THE SAFETY OF ACCOUNTABILITY TO SCRIPTURE AND PEOPLE

Christians aren't the only ones who pick up on things from the unseen realm. Nonbelievers often pick up unholy things in the spirit realm from their association with unclean spirits. People involved in the New Age philosophy identify these spirits as good or angelic, but Christians should identify them as demonic.

Hebrews 5:13, 14 stress the importance of knowing God's Word and using it in our daily lives. It is the way Christians train themselves to discern between good and evil. Any deceptive vision, dream or experience can be identified as such when it is filtered through the lens of Scripture. Living in accountability with other godly people will also keep us from wrongly interpreting a supernatural experience.

Application

1. What is your response to the different examples the author gave about how the Holy Spirit interacts with the spirit of a person and then filters the information through the soul and body?

2. Describe your experiences with hearing the voice of the Holy Spirit.

Chapter 5 Five

The Discernment of an Intercessor

The long hair and sloppy clothing were an indication to her that he might be searching for the Lord. "Have you given your whole life to the Lord?" she gently probed.

"Well . . . no," Peter replied.

"Would you like to?"

"Yes," he muttered.

The missionary then began to lead Peter in a prayer of repentance, salvation and dedication to the Lord. After interceding for him for a long while, she instructed Peter to destroy all his ungodly music. She warned him that old friends who had been a harmful influence on him needed to be replaced with Christian friends. She admonished Peter to make church attendance a habit and never again be involved with a girl sexually until marriage. The missionary assumed that she was moving in a word of knowledge for Peter.

Peter remained receptive and humble throughout this time of prayer. After all, he knew there were areas in his life that needed more of Jesus. It never occurred to him to stop this gracious lady and explain that he had been saved at a young age and attended church all of his life. He had led a large Bible study while in high school. Even now, most of his college friends were believers, and his choice in music continued to be Christian. He maintained a wholesome relationship with his fiancée, whom he planned to marry before he left for the mission field. Peter had answered honestly. He wanted his whole life filled with the Spirit of God—didn't every Christian?

Although no permanent damage was done, both the missionary and Peter missed what God wanted to do during that time of prayer. The missionary used her visual judgment of Peter's appearance and his simple replies to her questions to evaluate where he was spiritually. As a result, her "words from the Lord" for Peter were off-base. His reluctance to communicate only contributed to the missionary's misconceptions. She left the encounter believing that God had directed her intercession for Peter. He left without experiencing the deeper work of God that he longed for in his life.

It is not uncommon or unwise to ask questions when requested to pray for another. Nor do intercessors want to be oblivious to a person's countenance, because appearances are often indicators of a person's need. However, things of the spirit need to be evaluated at a deeper level than the five senses.

Discernment must also go beyond the soulish level of intellect, emotions and will. We all have a tendency to mistake our understanding of people for the voice of the Holy Spirit. We rely on personal knowledge of situations to determine direction in prayer. Our mind tells us that certain types of circumstances dictate certain prayer responses, and often our personal agenda for another becomes "God's will." Similarly, emotions have been known to masquerade as the direction of the Spirit.

Isaiah prophesied of Jesus that He would not judge by what He saw and heard. His evaluations would be based only on what the Holy Spirit communicated to Him:

> The Spirit of the Lord will rest on him—the Spirit of wisdom and of understanding, the Spirit of counsel and of power, the Spirit of knowledge and of the fear of the Lord. . . . He will not judge by what he sees with his eyes, or decide by what he hears with his ears (11:2, 3).

It is this same Spirit who comes to reside within each believer. His desire is to provide us with the things we need as emissaries for Christ: supernatural wisdom, understanding, counsel, power, knowledge and the fear of the Lord. Intercessors do not have to rely on their own observations and information, because the Holy Spirit will communicate the insight needed to intercede. He is constantly guiding us toward truth, advising us of the Father's directions:

> But when he, the Spirit of truth, comes, he will

guide you into all truth. He will not speak on his own; he will speak only what he hears, and he will tell you what is yet to come (John 16:13).

So how do we know if the inner things we are sensing are initiated by the Holy Spirit or just our own imagination and impulses? We all have known people who say, "The Lord told me . . ." and then we shudder at what they attribute to God. Many intercessors have experienced what they felt was a direct communication from the Lord, only to later realize it was their own opinion or need super-imposed over God's voice. Likewise, numerous intercession teams experience frustration when several members appear to be picking up different things from the Lord. They struggle over who is correctly hearing the Spirit's voice. Then there are those who just wonder if we ever hear from God at all!

Jesus stated that His sheep would know His voice apart from others (see John 10). He was relating to the manner in which a shepherd communicated with his flock. A shepherd doesn't drive and push his sheep as a cowboy herds cattle. He calls his sheep to follow him, and then leads them where he wants them to go. Several flocks of sheep are often bedded down together in a single sheep pen. In the morning, each shepherd calls his sheep out. Sheep know the voice of their shepherd and do not respond to the voice of other shepherds. If sheep can learn to distinguish the voice of their own shepherd from all the others, shouldn't we also be able to learn to differentiate the voice of our Shepherd from our opinions, the opinions of others, or the Enemy's impressions?

We have seen that God communicates with us mostly at the spirit level: His Spirit to our spirit. That communication is then filtered up through our soul and expressed through our body. Learning to discern between our soul and spirit is a lifelong process, and one in which we must constantly remain teachable. Intercessors need to study and practice this discerning process to be sensitive to things of the spirit realm. Examining the workings of our "soul-filter" will explain why we sometimes misinterpret what we hear from the Lord.

How the Soul-Filter Operates

In Matthew 5:8, Jesus promised that those with a pure heart would see God. That has always been the desire of an intercessor—to see God! This condition of a pure heart is met by avoiding sin and the things of the world that would dull our spiritual senses. Proverbs 4:23 counsels, "Above all else, guard your heart, for it is the wellspring of life."

Every farmer knows the importance of keeping the filter clean on the spring from which he gets his supply of water. A clogged filter causes impurities in the water that flows from the spring to the fields. Guarding our wellspring of life (our spirit) is much the same. If our soul-filter is full of debris, it can contaminate the Spirit of life that flows from us.

In chapter 3, we learned that our soul was designed to help us process the things of our spirit into the physical expressions of life. The soul works as a translator and a filter between our spirit, in contact with God's Spirit, and our body, in contact with the physical world. When the filter is clean, we find a clear transmission. When the filter is clogged or damaged, we find the transmission garbled between the Holy Spirit and ourselves.

We all know that a radio should easily pick up radio signals and translate those signals into clear, intelligible sound. But often all we hear is static. It is the same with our spirit, soul and body. Even though our spirit may distinctly hear God, the information doesn't always come through clearly because of static within the filter of our soul.

The static originates from our body and soul—erroneous thinking, hurt feelings, rebellion, and the use of our bodies in ways that Jesus has forbidden. It is the result of rubbish accumulated in areas where our soul has been impaired. Static crowds out "spirit signals" in receiving and transmitting from the Lord.

The following diagram was used during a teaching on restoration by Ken Pienka. I have made only a few adaptations to his excellent teaching for the purpose of this study. The visual explanation will supplement the instruction of this chapter.

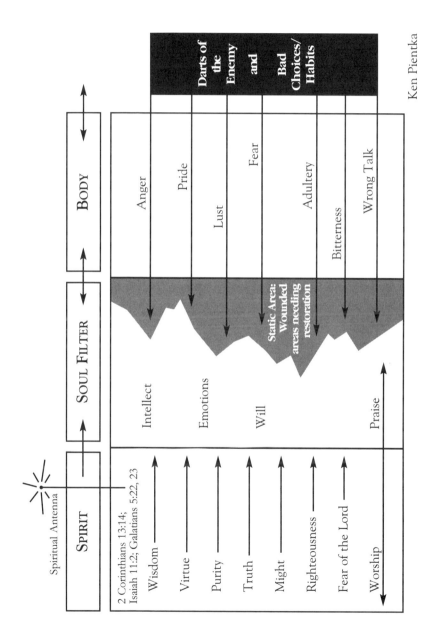

Ken Pientka

Spiritual Antenna

SPIRIT | **SOUL FILTER** | **BODY**

2 Corinthians 13:14;
Isaiah 11:2; Galatians 5:22, 23

Wisdom
Virtue
Purity
Truth
Might
Righteousness
Fear of the Lord
Worship

Intellect
Emotions
Will
Praise

Static Area:
Wounded areas needing restoration

Anger
Pride
Lust
Fear
Adultery
Bitterness
Wrong Talk

Darts of the Enemy and Bad Choices/ Habits

At salvation, the Holy Spirit comes to reside within our spirit and brings with Him the love of the Father, the grace of the Lord Jesus, and His desire to fellowship with us (see 2 Corinthians 13:14). Wisdom, understanding, counsel, and all the wonderful things mentioned in Isaiah 11:2 and Galatians 5:22, 23, are also deposited as seeds of righteousness. The Holy Spirit acts as a farmer, cultivating these seeds deep within us. Slowly, they begin to grow up out of our spirit and into our soul and body and eventually produce fruit—the fruit of the Spirit.

Ken explained that the more our soul is penetrated by these virtues, the more our soul becomes renewed. (Remember that our soul is in the process of being renewed, not re-created.) Our intellect, emotions and will begin to function under the rulership of the Lord and outwardly, change results.

THE CONSEQUENCE OF WOUNDS

Unfortunately, our soul also has areas where it has been wounded because of bad habits and sinful choices made throughout life. There are places where Satan's darts have penetrated and left us injured. Our soul may further bear the damage of the unrighteous words and actions of others. Consequently, the walls of our own personality have huge gaps in them where areas of our soul have been devastated. These broken walls of our personality become the building stones for enemy strongholds within our thoughts and emotions.

The massive walls of these fortresses obstruct the view of God that is needed for us to think, feel and act according to His dictates. Deception then counters the work of righteousness seeking to renew our soul. Usually, we are unable to identify these hidden walls of deception as anything other than the walls of our personality. They have been a part of us for so long we believe that they are, in reality, us! The result is continued unfruitfulness in certain areas of our life.

Untreated, these wounded areas and strongholds of deception clog up the filter of our souls and cause static, making it difficult to clearly hear the Holy Spirit. As a result, we often misinterpret our feelings or opinions for the voice of the Spirit. Sin and its wounds continue to cause distortion in how we process the things transmitted from our spirit up through our soul. They color our perception of different circumstances and dictate our reactions. Consider the following examples:

Mary found that her prayers for her teenagers were often colored by her overwhelming fear that they might be experimenting with drugs. After all, she had done a little experimentation herself when she was their age, why wouldn't they try it too? Her prayer times were apt to be verbal rehearsals of her fear rather than her faith. Mistakenly, she interpreted these fearful feelings as warning signals picked up by her spiritual antenna.

Jamie struggled with her prayer partner's inability to pray in a positive way about issues brought up during intercession. Her friend, Karen, always seemed to focus on the negative. Even more disturbing was the consistent message of doom, gloom and judgment that seemed to be woven throughout everything Karen heard from the Lord. Jamie suspected that the unresolved bitterness of Karen's divorce tended to distort the things she heard from God.

Years after Mike had been deeply hurt by his father, he found it difficult to rightly relate to his own children. He caught himself reacting to their childish ways with the same anger his father had displayed toward him. He grieved that his prayers for them seemed so shallow, but there wasn't anything he could do about it, it was as if his intercession for his kids was constantly being short-circuited.

All of us have sin-ravaged areas in our soul. These desolate places continue to produce the fleshly motives and actions of a sinful nature and provide a target for Satan's fiery darts. Recognizing this fact allows us to continue in intercession with a new alertness to our own areas of weakness, and gives us a compassion for the weaknesses of others. Static can therefore be expected but not embraced. It can act as a distress signal, alerting us to areas needing God's restoring work.

THE SIGNIFICANCE OF HEALING

Jesus is committed to the process of healing the damaged places of the soul. He uses time and many strategies to accomplish the inner restoration that is essential for the reclaiming of barren territory and the rebuilding of shattered walls within an individual. God has promised:

> Instead of bronze I will bring you gold, and silver in place of iron. Instead of wood I will bring you bronze, and iron in place of stones. I will make peace your governor and righteousness your ruler. No longer will violence be heard in your land, nor ruin or destruction within your borders, but you will call your walls Salvation and your gates Praise (Isaiah 60:17, 18).

God desires that every gap in our personal walls and every area of devastation in our souls be restored to wholeness. His words to Israel become our personal promise when He commits to rebuilding our walls with quality materials. The walls that define the restored areas of our personality are called salvation. They allow the rulership of peace, rightness of thinking, feeling and acting. No longer are violence, ruin or destruction allowed to define these areas of our personality. Praise is placed as a gate where restoration has been completed. What was once an area of static becomes a clean filter for the clear transmission between our spirit and the outside world.

Wounds hurt when they are touched; scars may hold memories, but there is no pain. We know an area has healed and the wall construction completed when we can respond with the fruit of the Spirit, where once we reacted unrighteously. A scar is all that remains of a former barren region which now blossoms with new growth. Scars are badges of wholeness and signal strength where previously there was weakness. Jesus will forever wear scars upon His hands and feet. So our areas of weakness become His strength to minister to others.

Rachel encountered nausea whenever she dressed for bed. Memories of past sexual abuse haunted both her intimate times with her husband and her attempts to pray concerning that area of their marriage. Her reputation as an intercessor hadn't been affected by this, since she avoided praying for anyone who might have the same problem. She didn't trust herself to hear from God when it came to matters of sexuality.

Bob, however, loved his wife and encouraged her to seek healing through one of the counselors at church. Reluctantly Rachel agreed. It took time, prayer and obedience to the suggestions of her counselor, but finally, Rachel was healed. Today, Rachel is known as someone who is strong in intercessory prayer for those wounded in sexual areas. Her ability to distinctly hear the Lord's voice in each situation is evidence that her soul-filter has been cleared of static in an area that once caused interference. Her weakness has become His strength.

Rachel's willingness to face her own areas of devastation made her a stronger intercessor. The things she learned could also be applied to other strongholds that faced her as a prayer warrior. The basic strategies are the same whether one is dealing with the inner walls of the personality, or strongholds within homes, churches, communities and nations. The process of tearing down strongholds and rebuilding spiritual walls will be discussed in a later chapter, so we will not elaborate on them here. At this point, it is sufficient to recognize that every intercessor faces static in hearing God's voice. Yet, static will be reduced as Jesus continues His work of restoring our soul.

Draw a diagram representing yourself, similar to the one given at the beginning of this chapter on the spirit, soul-filter and body.

1. On your diagram, copy the things identified in 2 Corinthians 13:14, Isaiah 11:2, Galatians 5:22, 23 and the other "seeds of righteousness" listed in the *spirit* section of the author's diagram. Identify and label the areas in your *soul-filter* section where these "seeds" have grown up out of your spirit and into your soul to produce the fruit of the Spirit.

2. In the *soul-filter* and *body* sections, identify, label and shade the areas where you have personally been wounded and need restoration. Use arrows to help define how much these wounds have infiltrated your soul. On the side of your diagram, note how these areas might cause static in your ability to clearly hear the Lord's voice.

3. Draw in the walls of salvation and the gates of praise where Jesus has completed restoration in different areas of your soul.

Chapter **6** Six

Fine-tuning the Inner Ear of an Intercessor

*E*arwax is a yellow or brown secretion that the glands of the ear canal produce. Normally this secretion causes no trouble. Occasionally, earwax will totally block an ear and cause partial deafness, making it difficult to hear those around us. A few drops of mineral oil in the affected ear removes the wax and restores hearing.

At times, an intercessor may find it difficult to hear the voice of the Holy Spirit. It could be that God is silent because He wants us to walk in what He has already told us to do. Or the difficulty in hearing could be the result of spiritual earwax clogging our "inner ear." Spiritual earwax is like the soul static we referred to in chapter 5. It causes some deafness and distorts the voice of the Holy Spirit. Removing soul static (or earwax) allows us to correctly transmit the voice of the Lord heard within our spirit. This is the first step in fine-tuning our inner ear.

The second step involves building up our inner person, so that we become people mighty in spirit. We are essentially created to rule by our spirits in harmony with the Holy Spirit. This means that our reasoning, emotions and choices of the soul should be subordinate to our spirit. They should reflect the Holy Spirit who lives within. It is the spirit that should be the dominant part of our person, not our soul. Becoming mighty in spirit involves exercising our spirit with spiritual disciplines, so that it might stretch and grow.

REMOVING INNER STATIC

1. *Pursue intimacy through prayer and repentance.* It would seem that prayer and repentance are obvious requirements for fine-tuning our inner ear. Still, it is amazing how much these areas are neglected. We generally lead such busy lives that we fail to notice when intimacy with the Lord has been inhibited. Whether or not we are aware of sin that might be causing interference in our relationship with God, the Holy Spirit is grieved.

The Holy Spirit longs for companionship with us. He waits for us to include Him in our internal musings. When sin hinders our discourse, He alerts us to its presence. It is the Holy Spirit who draws us with cords of love toward the Cross, where again we give to Jesus the sins for which He died. It is He who ignites the joy of our salvation deep within and strengthens our spirit. Choices to sin are individual, but choosing repentance always involves the alliance of the Holy Spirit. Repentance helps align our soul once again with our spirit and restores the intimacy with the Holy Spirit we've disregarded.

King David knew well the fellowship of the Holy Spirit and the love of the Father. However, it wasn't a life lived free of sin that caused God to call David a man after His own heart (see Acts 13:22). David had sinned greatly. He committed adultery with Bathsheba and then tried to hide it through murdering her husband. Only when confronted by the prophet Nathan did David understand that the impact of his sin had reached all the way to the throne of God. It was David's realization of broken intimacy that initiated the cry of Psalm 51:

> Against you, you only, have I sinned and done what is evil in your sight. . . . Create in me a pure heart, O God, and renew a steadfast spirit within me. Do not cast me from your presence or take your Holy Spirit from me. Restore to me the joy of your salvation and grant me a willing spirit, to sustain me (vv. 4, 10-12).

David's cry becomes the cry of intercessors whenever they realize that intimacy with the Lord has been cut off through sin. They desperately seek repentance and long for the Lord's presence. Intercessors aren't perfect, but they can actively fine-tune their inner ear through daily repentance and seeking the Holy Spirit's companionship.

2. *Utilize God's scalpel.* After repentance, the main ingredient required for fine-tuning the inner ear is the Word of God. It alone claims to be the agent for learning

how to discern between spirit, soul and body: "For the word of God is living and active. Sharper than any double-edged sword, it penetrates even to dividing soul and spirit, joints and marrow; it judges the thoughts and attitudes of the heart" (Hebrews 4:12).

God's Word is never without purpose. It never lies dormant within a person. Scripture placed within, through reading and meditation, becomes a living entity with a job description. This living and active Word of God is described as "sharper than any double-edged sword." We know that one side of that double-edged sword is wielded in battle during spiritual warfare. The other side is designed to be used as a scalpel—within us!

This scalpel is used to penetrate and separate our spirit, soul and body. It evaluates our thoughts and motives, exposing them as originating from our spirit or from wounded areas of our soul. All of us have experienced this scalpel. It hurts! Self-pity is cut away from tissue it has infected within our emotions and thoughts. Fear can be amputated when identified by scriptures such as 2 Timothy 1:7: "For God did not give us a spirit of timidity, but a spirit of power, of love and of self-discipline."

When the written Word becomes the living Word within a person, it creates a distinction between what is spirit, what is soul, and what are the five senses. Scripture has the ability to expose the garbage clogging our soul-filter. It also confirms the things of the Spirit of God. The more we study and apply the Word of God to our lives, the more we find ourselves able to discern between spirit, soul and body. Intercessors, therefore, fine-tune their inner ears by memorizing and meditating on the Word of God.

3. *Renew your mind.* When people transfer their citizenship from one country to another, they usually have to learn a new language and culture. They often begin with a translator to help them communicate in their new environment. Once they can speak the language themselves, they must learn the various philosophies and traditions characteristic of their new culture. They know that they have fully assimilated themselves into their new citizenship when they can think and reason totally in their new language. Their *self-talk* is no longer in the tongue of their birth, but in the language and mind-set of their new nationality.

When we become citizens of the kingdom of God, we also find it necessary to learn a new language and culture. The words of this new language may still be in our native tongue, but the ways of reasoning and viewing life are very different. To help us assimilate our new culture, we are given a book called the Word of God. It isn't enough that we simply read the Book to learn to speak correctly. We must also learn to process information according to the perspective of the author of the Book. Romans 12:2 explains it this way: "Do not conform any longer to the pattern of this world, but be transformed by the renewing of your mind. Then you will be able to test and approve what God's will is—his good, pleasing and perfect will."

Renewing the mind is not always easy. We unconsciously want to process information the way we have all of our life. Since our mind was not changed at salvation, it continues to think in patterns to which it has grown accustomed over many years. These ways of thinking are often in conflict with God's ways. For example, if your self-talk tended to be fearful when faced with difficulties, it isn't going to automatically become full of faith. Only a renewed mind will change thoughts of unworthiness to confidence. A judgmental or critical attitude doesn't change with salvation. It needs the readjustment of a renewed mind.

Old forms of thinking and reasoning account for a lot of static within the filter of our soul. They reflect the strongholds of deception that lie hidden within our personality. This makes it very difficult to distinguish God's will in any given situation. Obviously, it is important that intercessors know God's will if they are to pray accordingly!

Deceptive thoughts can be identified by listening to our self-talk. When wrong reasoning is recognized, it can be replaced with truth. Truth becomes the freeing agent in dismantling strongholds and replacing them with walls of salvation. God will use teaching, counseling and supernatural gifts to replace deception with truth, but each must always be based on His eternal truth—the Scriptures.

Renewing our mind involves saturating it with the Word and ways of God. If we want to know God's will, we must replace old patterns of thinking with God's patterns of thinking. This involves reading, assimilating and obeying the Word of God. Scripture is the only place where we find His character, actions and will revealed. Teaching, counseling, prophecy and word of knowledge must align with Scripture or they are invalid.

4. *Obtain an uninhibited heart.* Allowing ourselves to be uninhibited before the Lord cultivates a soul free of static. When he brought the ark of the Lord to the Tabernacle, King David danced before the Lord and all of Israel. His triumphant shouting and uninhibited dancing offended his wife, Michal, because her pride dictated what was acceptable worship both for herself and for others.

Consequently, Michal found herself barren for the rest of her life. David's uninhibited adoration before his God and his people left no place for the static of pride in his soul (see 2 Samuel 6:12-23).

To worship the Lord free of inhibitions will be different for each of us. For some, this involves physical freedom of expression such as singing, dancing or shouting. For others, it may be the quiet freedom of the heart that they find in solitude and meditation with the Father. Our places of fellowship provide different definitions of what is acceptable public worship, and these need to be respected. However, we can find our own places of abandonment to God within the perimeters of our private prayer closets.

I love to watch ice dancing on television, and someday I plan to use all those wonderful movements set to worship music as I dance before the Lord. But with the body I currently have, it would be physically impossible—too old and too heavy! So I do the next best thing—I put some worship music on the CD player, close my eyes, and use my imagination to unrestrainedly and gracefully dance before the Lord. Not only does the Lord love it, but it is great practice for my future performance!

We don't recognize how inhibited we are before the Lord until we check our reactions to the worship and prayer styles of others. Like Michal, we become offended and judge certain types of worship and prayer as unacceptable. This kind of pride only clogs up our soul-filter and eventually leads to spiritual barrenness within. As intercessors, we want to counter the static of pride by consistently striving for new levels and expressions of intimacy with our God.

5. *Cultivate humility.* One of the elements that fine-tunes the inner ear of an intercessor is humility, because humility invites God's grace. It is grace that brought salvation to us, and it is grace that sustains and carries us into eternity. Humility is the key to receiving the grace needed for clearly hearing the Lord's voice.

> All of you, clothe yourselves with humility toward one another, because, "God opposes the proud but gives grace to the humble." Humble yourselves, therefore, under God's mighty hand, that he may lift you up in due time (1 Peter 5:5, 6).

Pride brings opposition from God. This is the last thing an intercessor wants! When we are prideful, we tend to be unteachable and impressed with our importance and place in God's kingdom. We become self-centered and focused on our own opinions, feelings and desires. Inferiority and self-pity indicate a problem with pride because they, too, focus on "self." God opposes us when we get our focus off Him and onto ourselves.

In contrast, humility is not consumed with the awareness of one's self. Humble people find their identity and security only in the Lord Jesus. They can look at both their failures and victories and not dwell on either. The consuming focus of humble people is Jesus—His thoughts, feelings and desires. They are concerned with how Jesus would want them to think and act in any given situation. They pursue honesty with themselves, God and others. Their ambition is to rightly represent the Lord Jesus regardless of the cost. These people receive the grace needed to hear from God.

Bev is a people watcher. Not only does she watch, but she learns from people. She is content to learn, grow and serve as one of the background people within God's kingdom. She is often awakened late at night to pray for different individuals in the church. Interestingly, everyone goes to her for counsel and insight with their problems. Bev has cultivated humility in her life, and it has helped fine-tune her inner ear for clear reception of the Lord's dealings. The soul interference of pride or self-pity are not usually a problem in Bev's life.

6. *Practice submission.* Submission is a heart attitude before it is an outward action. A heart of submission counters the soul static of offense and rebellion and allows us to willingly adhere to the directions of those in authority over us. It also provides graciousness to acceptably disagree with those in authority when necessary, because our hearts are for and not against them.

There may come a time when disagreement is necessary if someone in authority is participating in serious sin or asking us to accept what is opposed to the kingdom of God. Our allegiance is first to God and then to our earthly authorities. If our gracious disagreement does not resolve the conflict, then we should follow the instructions in Matthew 18:15-17. If this does not work, then we must separate ourselves from that person. This might involve finding a new job or a new church. Whenever possible, seek to be under a person of authority who desires to relate to Jesus.

BUILDING UP OUR INNER PERSON TO BECOME MIGHTY IN SPIRIT

As we begin to understand the workings of our soul-filter, God begins to remove the accumulated debris that causes static. Over time, we learn to discipline ourselves so that our soul is able to function as the servant of our spirit. Building up our spirit is the second discipline that allows intercessors to discern between soul and spirit and effectively hear from God.

The enlarging of our spirit allows it to become the dominant part of our person. This involves exercising our spirit, which allows us to stretch our boundaries and grow. The building up of the spirit in an intercessor is essential in being led by the Spirit of God. The more our spirit is enlarged, the easier it is to recognize the Holy Spirit directing us. Practicing the following exercises will help develop and strengthen our spirit person and fine-tune our inner ear:

1. *Cultivate praying in the Spirit.* Being a Pentecostal believer has been of great benefit to me through what we classify as "praying in tongues"; some call it our prayer language. The passage in 1 Corinthians 14:2, 4, and 14 teaches us that when we are using our prayer language, we are speaking things that are mysteries or private information known only to God. It is a personal conversation between God and us. Our prayer language originates from our spirit. "For if I pray in a tongue, my spirit prays, but my mind is unfruitful" (v. 14).

The purpose of this kind of tongues is for communion with God and the edification, or building up, of our inner person (as opposed to prophecy, or tongues and interpretation, which edifies others). "For anyone who speaks in a tongue does not speak to men but to God. Indeed, no one understands him; he utters mysteries with his spirit .... He who speaks in a tongue edifies himself, but he who prophesies edifies the church" (vv. 2, 4).

When we use our prayer language, an unexplainable strength is imparted to our inner being. We may hesitate to acknowledge the importance of this activity because it is beyond our understanding, but it is vital to us who desire to be strong in spirit. When we pray in tongues we are exercising faith, because we have to bypass our understanding and rely on the Lord (see Jude 20). It is then that we find our spirit growing stronger. The more our spirit is built up, the more we are able to operate as spirit-motivated people.

2. *Expand your worship.* If you take another look at the diagram in chapter 5, you will notice that worship is placed within the spirit and praise is placed within the filter of the soul. This is because praise is an act of our will that prepares us for true worship. Worship is a response by our spirit to the Holy Spirit's revelation of Jesus Christ within us. Praise prepares our mind, emotions and body to express our spirit's response to the glory of Jesus.

According to John 4:24, authentic worship originates from within our spirit and is encompassed by truth: "God is spirit, and his worshipers must worship in spirit and in truth." It is the Holy Spirit who initiates worship within our spirit when we glimpse the awesomeness of our God. It is as we lay aside the things of our flesh, or unrenewed areas of our soul, that we are able to respond to the Holy Spirit. Philippians 3:3 explains it like this: "We who worship by the Spirit of God, who glory in Christ Jesus, and who put no confidence in the flesh."

Praise is different from worship in that praise is an act of our will, rather than a response to the inspiration of the Holy Spirit. In Psalm 42:5-11, we glimpse the inner workings of King David as his spirit asks questions of his soul: "Why are you downcast, O my soul? Why so disturbed within me?" He then commands his emotions to hope in God, his mind to remember the Lord, and his will to focus on praise. In Psalm 103, David again commands his soul and body to praise the Lord by using his mind to rehearse God's benefits and his mouth to speak praise. In each case David was bringing his soul and body into a place of obedience to praise the Lord. Praise keeps our soul and body from blocking true worship, which originates in our spirit.

This explains why we usually begin a time of worship in church or a prayer meeting with praise. We need a transition interval of praise to readjust our mind, emotions and will to focus on the Lord, rather than the things of everyday life. Do you ever find it difficult to concentrate on the Lord at church after an argument with your teen? How often have you been singing songs of praise with other believers but thinking about dinner or the afternoon sports telecast? Like David, our soul requires time to align itself to be the servant of our spirit. Once that happens, worship can freely be expressed by our spirit, soul and body.

To exalt the Lord means to magnify Him, or bring Him into closer view. When we worship the Lord, we are seeing Him as greater than anything else we face. The pressures and cares of life become smaller in comparison to His glory. This is why worship is so significant in the enlarging of our spirit. Expanding our worship forces our spirit to grow. It must now adapt to the bigger vision we are receiving of Jesus. When Jesus becomes magnified within us, we become bigger people as a result.

3. *Nourish your spirit with Spirit food.* If our spirit is to grow, it must be nourished. In John 6:63, Jesus identified spirit nourishment as follows: "The words I have spoken to you are spirit and they are life." As a dinner meal nourishes our body, the Word of God nourishes our spirit. His Word, which is Spirit, can generate life at the very core of our being.

My grandmother Bessie David lived out the final years of her life in a nursing home. She loved to sing the old hymns full of Scripture long after she failed to recognize her children and grandchildren. Her mind was gone, but her spirit was alive and active. I often found her sharing the gospel with other patients, even though she couldn't remember who I was or why I was there. Passages of Scripture memorized long ago would come pouring from her at the slightest encouragement. Grandma had fed her spirit the right kind of food, and the life of God continued to be displayed even after her body and soul began to fail. Bessie had been an intercessor, mighty in spirit, who prayed her family into the Kingdom.

The Book of Hebrews describes this nourishment both as baby's milk for new believers and as solid food for the more mature:

> We have much to say about this, but it is hard to explain because you are slow to learn. In fact, though by this time you ought to be teachers, you need someone to teach you the elementary truths

of God's word all over again. You need milk, not solid food! Anyone who lives on milk, being still an infant, is not acquainted with the teaching about righteousness. But solid food is for the mature, who by constant use have trained themselves to distinguish good from evil (5:11-14).

Intercessors aren't to remain immature, focusing only on the basic truths of their faith. They must go on to study and practice what the Bible says about right relationships with God and with others. Head knowledge without life application cannot produce spirit growth. The Word of God must consistently be used as a scalpel on attitudes and motives. It must constantly replace old thought patterns with Kingdom thought patterns. Only then will a Christian be trained to discern good from evil. Intercessors need to be mighty in spirit, able to discern good and evil with their spirit, rather than with their soul or five senses. By building up their spirit through the nourishment and use of Scripture, they acquire that discernment.

As the filter of the soul is cleansed and the spirit enlarged, an intercessor will find it easier to recognize the Holy Spirit directing his or her spirit. Confidence is built as the inner ear is fine-tuned. Even the silent times of waiting for God's direction become growing experiences. Participating in intercession becomes an ongoing learning process. Just as Isaiah prophesied of Jesus, an intercessor can say of the Lord, "He wakens me morning by morning, wakens my ear to listen like one being taught" (Isaiah 50:4).

Application

1. Explain in your own words the various disciplines discussed in this chapter needed to remove soul static. Which of these need to be developed in your life?

2. Explain in your own words the various disciplines discussed in this chapter that are needed to enlarge your spirit.

Part II

The Practice of Intercession

Supplicant, Warrior and Watchman

Holding my baby close, I paced the floor praying. His fever was high as I again petitioned the Lord to bring relief to my son. This was the second night in a row I had been up with him. Somehow I knew this sickness was a spiritual attack against our fledgling ministry in a church where witches had attended our first service. Turning again toward the living room, I saw a vision of a bright ball of light in the hallway. As I walked toward it repeating the name of Jesus, it darted over to the window. Still holding my baby, I again approached it in the name of Jesus. It left by way of the window. Immediately, my baby slept peacefully without a fever.

The intercession I had done that night tied together two abilities: the ability to perceive things in the spirit realm and the ability to petition the Lord for healing. A simple act of spiritual warfare brought my intercession to a close. My task was completed and my baby was healed.

The Bible gives us three pictures to help us better understand the task of an intercessor. The first is of a man standing in the gap as a *supplicant*, the second is of a *warrior*, and the third is the illustration of a *watchman*. Each picture revolves around the understanding of the purpose of city walls during Biblical times, and how those walls defined and protected the city.

THE WALLS OF A CITY

Ancient cities usually had a wall built around them to protect the inhabitants from intruders. Assailants would seek to break down part of the wall by digging tunnels under the walls to weaken the foundations. Wooden gates could be set afire, providing an opening for enemy troops to enter. Many armies used battering rams to destroy the walls of a city; or, if the walls were limestone, they could be crumbled by the heat of large fires placed against them. The resulting gap left an unprotected breach in the city's defenses. The defenders would rush to hold back the invaders, while at the same time rebuilding the walls. If no one was available to rebuild the wall or stand in its gap, the city would be destroyed.

In Nehemiah 4, we find the story of the rebuilding of Jerusalem's walls during a time of threatening opposition. Nehemiah positioned half of his men as warriors around the walls, while the other half rebuilt the gaps caused by years of war and neglect. Those assigned as builders worked with one hand and held a weapon in the other.

Because the work was spread over a vast area, watchmen were posted to sound a trumpet if a workplace came under attack and needed aid.

In Ezekiel's time, the Lord used the illustration of broken walls to describe Israel's spiritual rebellion, sin and corruption. Her spiritual walls had huge gaps that resulted in the invasion of unholy philosophies and practices. The nation was decaying spiritually, and all sorts of enemies were ransacking her people. God was set to destroy Israel if the nation didn't recognize its decadence and turn again to His ways. Israel needed someone to stand in the gap, plead for mercy and rebuild her spiritual walls, but there was no intercessor. The Lord said, "I looked for a man among them who would build up the wall and stand before me in the gap on behalf of the land so I would not have to destroy it, but I found none" (Ezekiel 22:30).

Francis Frangipane has described a *gap* as the distance between the way things are and the way things ought to be.[1]

There are many situations in peoples' lives and in the life of our nation where a gap has appeared. We can see that things are not right. Sometimes these breaches are caused by personal sin; other times they are the result of another's sin. Whatever the case, these gaps provide an opening for evil or for the judgment of God (or both). It is an intercessor's task to stand in the gap to (1) plead for God's mercy and intervention and (2) to fight as spiritual warriors against the invasion of evil. The first is called *supplication*; the second is *spiritual warfare*.

STANDING IN THE GAP AS A SUPPLICANT

Supplication can be described as asking or petitioning another for mercy. Psalm 106:23 gives us the example of Moses as a supplicant for the nation of Israel: "So
[God] said he would destroy them—had not Moses, his
chosen one, stood in the breach before him to keep his
wrath from destroying them." Exodus 32, 33 give us a
fuller picture of the role of a supplicant as more than
just one who begs for God's mercy. The story is a familiar one. Moses goes up Mount Sinai to meet with God,
and Aaron builds a golden calf for the people to worship. God becomes angry and states His intention to
destroy the people. At this point Moses begins to plead
with God to spare the nation, but his cries are more
than "Please, please, please don't hurt them."

Moses begins by recalling God's involvement and
rescue of His people from Egypt. He then brings up
God's reputation as leverage and continues by recalling
the promises God made to Abraham and his descendants. After this very judicial argument, God relents in
His plan to destroy the nation (32:11-14). There is one
stipulation to His decision: He will allow the people to
proceed to their destination but without Him (33:3).
Moses panics! What good are God's promises if His presence is absent? Moses launches into one of the most serious, yet humorous, supplications in the Bible:

> Moses said to the Lord, "You have been telling
> me, 'Lead these people,' but you have not let me
> know whom you will send with me. You have
> said, 'I know you by name and you have found
> favor with me.' If you are pleased with me, teach

me your ways so I may know you and continue to find favor with you. Remember that this nation is your people" (33:12, 13).

So far, so good. Moses quotes the Lord and then draws on those statements to focus on the future, ending with a reminder that, after all, these are *Your* people; this was *Your* idea! The logical dispute immediately has God's reply, "My Presence will go with you, and I will give you rest" (v. 14).

Such reassurance should have ended the discussion. Yet, Moses is so involved in the argument that he keeps plowing relentlessly ahead:

> If your Presence does not go with us, do not send us up from here. How will anyone know that you are pleased with me and with your people unless you go with us? What else will distinguish me and your people from all the other people on the face of the earth? (vv. 15, 16).

Again the Lord reassures Moses of His presence and favor. Moses still isn't satisfied. He boldly asks to see God's glory! (v. 18). Now that's supplication!

Note that Moses was respectful with God but unafraid to state his case with boldness and emotion. According to Hebrews 4:16, we have that same right: "Let us then approach the throne of grace with confidence, so that we may receive mercy and find grace to help us in our time of need." An intercessor will approach the throne of God to plead the case of another with confidence and determination. This is actually giving honor to the One who has called us to rule and reign with Him (see Romans 5:17).

God never changes His mind concerning His character, rules and goals, but He will change His mind concerning people. When a holy God meets an unholy person, something has to change; and it isn't God! The Lord has choices in His dealings with people. It is people who are the deciding factor. In the case of Moses and the nation of Israel, it was the people who made a choice to turn away from God. They had been chosen as the nation that God would nurture until, through them, He brought forth His Son. Their decision to rebel left God with two choices: to either continue toward His goal of redemption with a rebellious nation or start a new nation with Moses (see Exodus 32:10). The tenacious intercession by Moses changed God's mind, but not His character, rules or goal.

Intercessors have the privilege of standing in the gap as a supplicant before God on behalf of others. That requires obedience, respect, and an understanding of the purposes and goals of God in bringing His kingdom life to people and situations. Advocates also need tenacity to stand in the gap for as long as it takes to present their case in a logical manner based upon God's promises and character.

STANDING IN THE GAP AS A WARRIOR

The second purpose of an intercessor who stands in the gap is that of spiritual warfare. In this arena intercessors do not face God in prayer as they did in supplication. They turn and face the forces of evil and war against them. The warrior's role is one of enforcing Christ's victory, which was won at Calvary.

Jesus won the right to the hearts of people through His work on the cross; Satan was the loser.

> When you were dead in your sins and in the uncircumcision of your sinful nature, God made you alive with Christ. He forgave us all our sins, having canceled the written code, with its regulations, that was against us and that stood opposed to us; he took it away, nailing it to the cross. And having disarmed the powers and authorities, he made a public spectacle of them, triumphing over them by the cross (Colossians 2:13-15).

Unfortunately, Satan didn't take defeat lying down. He still seeks to steal, kill and destroy the lives of people all over the world (John 10:10). His attacks are in direct defiance to Christ's victory and usually take the form of guerrilla warfare. Jesus Christ has authorized us to enforce His kingdom rule against the forces of evil in the spirit realm, as we take His gospel to the physical nations of the earth. Jesus said to us: "All authority in heaven and on earth has been given to me. Therefore go and make disciples of all nations . . . " (Matthew 28:18, 19).

According to Mark 16, anything that gets in the way of "going and making disciples" comes under the authority given us by Jesus:

> Go into all the world and preach the good news to all creation. Whoever believes and is baptized will be saved, but whoever does not believe will be condemned. And these signs will accompany those who believe: In my name they will drive

> out demons; they will speak in new tongues; they
> will pick up snakes with their hands; and when
> they drink deadly poison, it will not hurt them at
> all; they will place their hands on sick people,
> and they will get well (vv. 15-18).

Authority over hell (driving out demons), authority over natural limitations (speaking in new tongues), authority over the animal creation (picking up snakes), authority over natural laws (drinking deadly poison), and authority over sickness have all been delegated to the believer who acts in the name of Jesus as His representative. (For several examples of this authority in action, read Acts 8:4-8 and 28:1-10.)

We might compare the task of an intercessor to the work of a policeman. It is the assignment of the local police to enforce the laws of the land in a community where some refuse to recognize the authority of the United States government. Satan refuses to recognize the work of the Cross wherever he can deceive people into believing that it didn't happen. Our job is to remind Satan of his defeat and refuse him the right to operate illegally. When the name of Jesus and the authority of His work and Word are brought against Satan, he and his forces must cease their work of destruction.

Ephesians 6:12 identifies these forces as rulers, authorities and powers operating in the heavenly or spirit realms. These rulers of darkness continue to resist us as we move forward in the plans of God. Jesus stated, "From the days of John the Baptist until now, the kingdom of heaven has been forcefully advancing, and forceful men lay hold of it" (Matthew 11:12).

Intercessors are those forceful warriors who willingly fight for the progress of God's kingdom. This kingdom is unseen, and its boundaries are in the hearts of people. At every outpost there are intercessors fighting for the continued advancement of the gospel. Not only do they refuse the Enemy the right to gain entrance through a breach in a wall, but they push his forces back and lay hold of territory once occupied by him. Because of the faithfulness of intercessors, God's kingdom walls are ever expanding.

Intercessors stand in the gap and war for another, so that God's purposes become reality in that person's life. They fight for their churches and communities in the spirit realm with weapons and strategies that might appear unusual to others. Their battles take place in the heavenlies, but their victories are seen by all. God has provided an intercessor with armor, weapons and strategies to use against the Enemy, as well as insights into His nature and battle plans.

STANDING IN THE GAP AS A WATCHMAN

A final picture is that of a watchman. The basic unit of the church is the family. Intercessors usually begin their ministry by learning to stand in the gap for their family and discovering how to watch upon the spiritual walls of their household. In Bible times a watchtower was placed within a pasture, orchard or vineyard as a location from which a man could watch for wild animals or thieves that might endanger his animals or crops. The livelihood of a man and the security of his household depended upon how well a watchman did his job.

As intercessors, many of us watch upon the spiritual walls of our families, keeping vigil against an unseen enemy. Through the eyes of the spirit, we are able to sight impending danger and sound an alarm when needed. Sometimes there is a gap in the wall where stones have shifted and fallen into disarray. At that point we must leave our watchtower, stand in the gap and engage in spiritual warfare.

Each walled city of long ago also had watchtowers built upon their corners. Watchmen could see a great distance from these towers to alert the city if an enemy approached. Anyone drawing near who indicated hostile intent was reported to the king or the elders of the city. The night watch was often the most dangerous, and a watchman needed to be especially vigilant. Likewise, intercessors must be especially alert during times of spiritual darkness.

Many intercessors are called to be watchmen for their churches or other Christian organizations. Their duties as sentries include keeping a vigilant eye out for danger and reporting anything unusual to their superiors. The things they sense in the spirit are like the field reports of top-notch spies. Consequently, they are often the eyes and ears for busy leadership who may not have noticed the advancement of Enemy forces.

Watchmen also had the privilege of announcing the arrival of important ambassadors and dignitaries (see Isaiah 52:7, 8). Two New Testament watchmen saw the coming of the Messiah and, on the day of His arrival in Jerusalem, both Anna and Simeon announced His entry to all who would listen (see Luke 2:25-38). The promise of a Messiah, given so long before, had finally arrived in the form of a baby. The role of a watchman involves both watching for danger and announcing the arrival of the promises of God. God sets watchmen in their place upon the walls and He requires that they take their job seriously (see Isaiah 62:6, 7).

BLENDING THE THREE ROLES OF AN INTERCESSOR

It is interesting that spiritual giftings fall naturally into one of the three tasks of an intercessor. For example, a person with the gift of mercy will gravitate toward the supplicant role, as will the encourager. Like Moses, their heart is for God's intervention of grace in the lives of sinners. Those with a pastor's heart will lean toward the role of the warrior, because they want to protect their sheep. Those with an evangelistic or missionary heart will also favor the warrior side of intercession because their desire is to see God's kingdom expanded.

A prophet often functions best in the role of watchman, because they can see things afar off and warn those who need to heed their message. Like Jonah, they may find it difficult to stand in the supplicant's place and plead for those they warn. This doesn't mean that they shouldn't intercede as a supplicant, because all have the duty to fulfill all three of the roles of an intercessor. But they will normally fill one role more efficiently than another.

As intercessors, we may be called upon to stand in the gap as a supplicant before the Lord on behalf of another. Other times we will rise in the radiant armor of a warrior to face a spiritual foe who would seek to destroy the people or work of God. Finally, we stand as a watchman alert upon the walls of our city or vineyard as we scan the spiritual horizon for enemy activity or the advent of one of God's promises. We may function in one or more of these roles during a session of intercession. It all depends on how the Holy Spirit is directing the time of prayer.

Intercessors begin their time of prayer by submitting themselves to the Lord. This is the first phase of the James 4:7 format of submitting ourselves to God, resisting the devil and seeing him flee. Submission involves repenting of any known sin in our lives and putting on our spiritual armor. Seasoned intercessors have learned to always be clothed in their armor and be ready in any crisis to step into battle. This preparation can begin early in the day if we are going to participate on a team or in corporate intercession.

Intercession includes sharpening our sword by reviewing any scriptures the Lord brings to mind for the time of intercession. Praise and worship are essential when intercessors stand before the throne of God. As we discussed in chapter 5, Isaiah 60:18 states that we are to call our walls *salvation* and our gates *praise*. His salvation surrounds us like the walls of a fortress.

Our spiritual gates in these walls are called *praise* and control what enters and exits our "city of intercession." The gates are where the city government meets and councils of war are convened. What comes in and out of our spiritual walls, individually or as a team, is expressed in praise and our counsel for war is received at the gates of praise. The Lord's agenda for spiritual warfare is usually received during praise and worship.

From this point, supplicants remain before the throne to present their petitions before the Father. Their work requires that their attention be focused on the Judge of all the earth. Many times, intercession goes no further. Other times, intercession moves into the phase of resisting the Enemy. It is often during "high praise" that the transition happens. Warriors turn from the throne to face the forces of darkness.

> Let the high praises of God be in their mouth, and a two-edged sword in their hand, to execute vengeance on the nations, and punishment on the peoples; to bind their kings with chains, and their nobles with fetters of iron; to execute on them the judgment written; this is an honor for all His godly ones. Praise the Lord! (Psalm 149:6-9, NASB).

God has declared judgment against His enemies and it is the warrior's privilege to enforce that judgment. Various expressions of the sword of the Spirit are utilized from a warrior's spiritual arsenal as they engage an enemy resisting God's mandates. It is not flesh and blood the warrior faces but spiritual forces of evil. God promises that a warrior's resistance will cause the Enemy to flee.

The role of a watchman is intermingled throughout the two phases of intercession. We see things during our time of submitting before the Lord. Other times, we mount our watchtower in the midst of a battle to gain an overall view of the conflict. Our work supports both supplication and warfare.

Individuals should transit easily among all three roles of an intercessor. Teams should feel comfortable pausing to discuss what they are seeing from their watchtowers or sensing for each phase of intercession. Corporate

intercession also involves both these phases with intercessors combining their efforts as supplicants, warriors
and watchmen.

1. Throughout the kingdom of God, intercessors are
rising as supplicants, warriors and watchmen for their families, churches and worldwide evangelism. In your own
words, summarize the various activities of an intercessor:
supplicant, warrior and *watchman.*

2. How have you experienced the combination of
all three roles of supplicant, warrior and watchman
in your times of intercession? In which role are you
most comfortable?

Chapter 8 Eight

The Base Camp of an Intercessor

"I think my wife has a demon, can you help us?" The voice on the other end of the phone sounded desperate. "We have called almost every church in the area and all we get is answering machines or the comment that they don't believe in demons."

I assured the young man that, yes, we did believe in demons, and my husband would be glad to help if they would drive over to the church. It was Saturday night and Tom was studying for his sermon the next morning. I thought he might appreciate the diversion!

Tom listened as Jim explained how his wife had become involved in automatic handwriting in an attempt to contact her dead father. Carolyn now had no control of her hands. They would involuntarily write out messages in the air if she didn't provide paper and pencil. As a backslidden Christian, Jim knew he needed to get his terrified wife to someone who could cast out demons.

For the next two hours, Tom confronted the demonic stronghold that had taken over Carolyn's life. At times, the demon would snarl like a wolf or throw Carolyn to the floor. Never touching her or entering into a dialogue with the demon, my husband calmly commanded it to leave in the name of Jesus. He reminded the demon of Christ's victory at Calvary and insisted that it adhere to the terms of that conquest. At the end of this encounter, Carolyn was a free woman. Today she serves as the director of Women's Ministries of the church we pastor.

It had taken Jim and Carolyn half an hour to get from their house to the church. That brief time allowed Tom to go before the Lord in intercession and review the Scriptures that taught of Christ's victory. Revisiting Calvary had become a habit for Tom. It was there his vision was clarified, and the voice of the Spirit was easier to hear. By the time Jim and Carolyn walked in the door, Tom was confident that Jesus would once again be glorified in someone's life.

PITCH YOUR TENTS

From my childhood I have known the ageless story of Jesus and the cross. Every Easter I have heard the narrative of the Crucifixion and Resurrection. Now, as a mother, I recite it to my children. I know the words and the reality that "Jesus died for my sins"; but my familiarity has resulted in distance. This ought not to be so for an intercessor.

The cross of Calvary must be both familiar and close.

We must learn its power and significance because everything an intercessor is and does revolves around the accomplishment of Jesus Christ and the Cross. It is through Calvary's binoculars that a watchman greets the promises of God (see 2 Corinthians 1:20). A supplicant bases intercession on the truth and grace that was released there (see John 1:17). The warrior boldly enforces the victory won by Jesus on that "old rugged cross." Even the uniform and weapons of an intercessor were bought at Calvary.

We are about to become involved in the greatest battle since Calvary—that which precedes the return of the King. Intercessors must understand that the ground on which they stand is stained crimson with the blood of Almighty God. Only from this position can they proceed in authority against a deadly and determined foe. Therefore, at the foot of the Cross is where an intercessor sets up base camp. Only there do we gain understanding of the price Jesus paid to redeem humanity from the sin of Adam.

KNOW YOUR ORIGINS

Adam had been given a beautiful world to cultivate and a wife to love and cherish. But Satan came into this lovely garden and tempted Adam to disobey the conditions of rulership over earth. Adam's wife, Eve, had already been deceived by Satan, but Adam was not (see 1 Timothy 2:14). He knew exactly what he was being asked to do—disobey the God who loved him.

Adam knew that if anyone ate the fruit of the Tree of Knowledge of Good and Evil, the consequences would be death (Genesis 2:17). Adam's choice brought sin and death into a world that had not been designed for evil. His sin provided legal entry for Satan and his forces to make earth a stronghold of darkness. The contamination of sin was then passed from Adam to each succeeding generation.

KNOW GOD'S SACRIFICE

God was grieved at Adam's rejection of His love, for He passionately adored this man and his wife. He knew that something must be done with the problem of sin so that He might again enjoy an intimate relationship with humanity. He began by killing an animal and using the skin to cover Adam and Eve's nakedness (Genesis 3:21). Its blood would hide their sin from the eyes of God for only a short time. He then taught them the importance of sacrificing a blameless animal so that blood would continue to be a sin covering. They, in turn, taught their children (see 4:1-7).

Only innocent blood could cover sin. The principle would be clarified in the instructions given to Moses for the nation of Israel. That nation became a walking example of God's unfolding plan of redemption. In due time John the Baptist identified Jesus as "the Lamb of God, who takes away the sin of the world!" (John 1:29). The Lamb had finally arrived who would become the complete sacrifice for all of the human race.

God's love for people became the driving force behind an awesome strategy to free humanity from sin. His love also demanded that the one who introduced sin to the human race would be judged. Satan and his forces would no longer have power over those freed from sin. Therefore, innocent blood from a sinless man would be required to pay for the sins of humankind and redeem the ownership of humanity held by Satan. This two-pronged strategy converged at a place called Calvary.

Calvary was the one time in all of eternity past where God the Father and God the Spirit were separated from God the Son. We mortals do not comprehend the enormity of this. God loved us so much He altered His own Trinity relationship to free us from sin and from Satan. He who had always been God chose to also become man. Only a God-man could represent both divinity and humanity in the courts of heaven (see Job 9:32, 33; 1 Timothy 2:5). The Son willingly confined Himself to a human body, yet without sin, so that He might be killed. Only as a human could God experience death, since death was something reserved for flesh and blood.

All of the sins of the human race were placed upon the God-man as He hung on the cross—from the first dis-obedience by Adam until the future Great White Throne Judgment (see 1 John 2:2; Hebrews 2:9). Every sin that you and I have and will commit was heaped upon Jesus: bad thoughts, offenses, self-pity, anger, murder, rejection, lies and bitterness. Every horror that Hitler, Lenin and other masters of evil would commit were also bestowed upon our Lord. Jesus took Adam's original sin and the sins of each person who has ever, or will ever, live and made those sins His own. He became total sin.

There, on a lonely cross, Jesus took on the sins of the world so that in His death sin would also die. It was the only way that humanity could again become right before God (2 Corinthians 5:21). He who had cursed man with death now experienced it Himself (Galatians 3:13). God the Father and God the Holy Spirit turned away from

God the Son, who in His innocence became crucified Sin. In His holiness, God walked away from a cross. In His love, God the Son embraced the cross so that we might be ransomed (John 10:17, 18).

As this innocent Lamb shed His blood, our sins became invalid in the courts of heaven. Neither could death hold Him in the grave, for sin and its death-curse were rendered powerless. He rose triumphant to proclaim freedom to all men who would accept His redeeming work (see 1 Timothy 4:10). Heaven rang with the declaration that sin and Satan no longer had legal authority over man, for the price of innocent blood had been eternally paid (Romans 6:6; Hebrews 2:14, 15). Our Lamb forever stands beside the throne as One who has been freshly slain (Revelation 5:6, 12; 7:17; 13:8).

KNOW YOUR ASSIGNMENT

In the spirit realm, the Cross still stands to declare the triumph of Jesus Christ over sin. It is the place each person must first visit to enter the kingdom of God. This is where ownership of one's life is transferred to God's ownership through repentance. The force of sin is then officially broken. Christians know the personal nature of this place as they revisit it any time they need to apply its power over sin. Repentance continues to declare freedom for a believer. Moreover, the lure of temptation is resisted by those who live under Calvary's shadow.

Supplicants intercede for those who are not experiencing freedom from sin. Their heart cry is for an increase of truth and grace over the one for whom they pray. Although "the truth will set you free" (John 8:32), it must be surrounded by grace or its revelation becomes legalistic and causes damage. The uniqueness of the Cross is that both truth and grace continually flow from it to a sinful world (John 1:17). This is part of a supplicant's stance—praying that the power of the Cross would shatter sin's hold over individuals.

Furthermore, the Cross declares the triumph of Jesus Christ over evil spirits. Powers of darkness have been defeated and have no authority. The final judgment against Satan has been declared, although its penalty will not be carried out until after Christ Jesus returns to Planet Earth. In the meantime, Christ's church has been assigned the responsibility of enforcing the victory of Calvary wherever the forces of darkness ignore its decree. Intercessors act as a spiritual police force sent into hostile situations. Through prayer, they require demons to comply with the terms of victory declared at Calvary.

Satan and his demons feed on people's ignorance of Calvary by masquerading as true authority. This charade gives them entrance into the lives of people and nations. Only when God's spiritual police force arrives to enforce Calvary's rule are they exposed and removed. Spiritual warfare involves skirmishes. This is part of a warrior's stance—refusing to relinquish the position of freedom gained through Christ's victory at the Cross.

Every promise in Scripture that is brought to the attention of a watchman by the Holy Spirit was bought for them at Calvary. These promises allow a person to share in the divine nature of God and help them escape corruption (2 Peter 1:4). On the basis of Christ's redemptive work, an intercessor can grab hold of such a promise and pray for its release in a person's life (see 2 Corinthians 1:20). This is part of a watchman's stance—refusing to relinquish the promises of God revealed to them by the Holy Spirit.

The supplicant, warrior and watchman all wage the fight of faith. We are commanded to "fight the good fight of faith, lay hold on eternal life, whereunto thou art also called, and hast professed a good profession before many witnesses" (1 Timothy 6:12, KJV). This battle is called *good* because it is one of enlarging our belief in the finished work of Calvary. It is only through faith in Christ's work that supplicants can see a person set free from sin. Faith is the shield that covers warriors as they confront a spirit enemy operating illegally. Watchmen must use the binoculars of faith every time they scan the horizon.

Sin has been conquered. Satan has been defeated. The judgment against him has been pronounced (see John 1:12; Acts 16:30). The commission to every believer has been assigned:

> Then Jesus came to them and said, "All authority in heaven and on earth has been given to me. Therefore go and make disciples of all nations, baptizing them in the name of the Father and of the Son and of the Holy Spirit, and teaching them to obey everything I have commanded you. And surely I am with you always, to the very end of the age" (Matthew 28:18-20).

Intercessors carry this commission into the spirit realm through the activity of prayer. Mercy and grace are sought for others because of the work of the Lamb. Demonic principalities and powers are confronted by the authority bought by the Lamb's blood. The promises of God are theirs only because Jesus Christ willingly shed His blood at Calvary.

That blood forever stains the ground at the foot of the Cross. This ground is where intercessors pitch their tents. It becomes their base camp. From there they receive daily assignments; they enter the throne room to make their pleas before the Father; they march forth into battle. From this base camp, they mount their watchtower to scan the horizon. And it is from there that they will one day step from earth's shadows into heaven's reality.

It is the Cross of Jesus Christ that stands as the entrance to all things in the kingdom of God.

Application

1. Why is it important for an intercessor to be intimately acquainted with the work of Calvary?

2. Make a list, with Scripture references, of what was accomplished by Christ's death on the cross. This list and its accompanying scriptures will serve as a reference library when you prepare your supplications or watch for the promises of God. It will also become your legal search and seizure warrant against the forces of evil and their strongholds.

3. Why do we often find it difficult to *fight the good fight of faith*? How has this fight enlarged your belief in the finished work of Calvary?

Chapter *9* Nine

Reconnaissance

*E*ntering the throne room, Gabriel and Michael walked toward the Commander in Chief. The place was bustling with angels and the redeemed, who had passed from life on earth to their home in heaven. Joy, dancing and an awesome sense of holiness permeated the atmosphere. An overall sense of order orchestrated the worshipers. Gabriel nudged Michael toward the side of the throne when he saw that Jesus was busy with a group of intercessors. They would wait until He was done with these important people.

It had always impressed the angels to find these people, who still lived on earth, gathered around the Savior. It had something to do with the Scripture passage that said they had been raised with Christ and seated with Him in the heavenly realms (see Ephesians 2:6). With

Christ, they were "far above all rule and authority, power and dominion, and every title that [could] be given" (1:20-22). Apparently, this position allowed them to view situations on earth from the perspective of heaven. Though not physically present, these believers still had rights to the throne the angels didn't.

The two angels listened to Jesus direct the gaze of His watchmen and explain His varied battle plans to His warriors. They noticed that He joined in the supplication of those who had come to plead for mercy from the Father. At times the group was very serious, yet often they laughed as Jesus pointed out the bewilderment of their defeated Enemy. The war had already been won. Their job was to declare its victory to those who still lived under the illegal rulership of Satan. It was because freedom needed to be proclaimed to those still in bondage that these intercessors regularly gathered at the throne.

Never leaving the intercessors, Jesus turned toward the two angels. Their work would now be combined with that of the intercessors. They listened intently as their Commander in Chief outlined the next advance of troops into Enemy-occupied territory.

Reconnaissance is the examination of territory for military operations. It involves scouting out enemy fortifications and artillery as well as possible points of invasion. Intercessors spend much time beside the throne doing reconnaissance work with Jesus. They know that when the Savior walked the earth, He only did those things He saw His Father doing (John 5:19). How much more must they now see with the Lord's eyes and only do what He initiates!

Acquire a Heavenly Perspective

Believers often are either oblivious to the workings of the Enemy or they exaggerate his power. If Satan can deceive people into believing he doesn't exist and isn't a threat to their family, then he can operate in anonymity. If this approach fails, he will attempt to deceive people into believing that hell's forces are all-powerful and a foe against which there is little hope. Intercessors must not fall prey to either of these lies. Their job involves unmasking the deceptions of demons by exalting the work of Calvary. Therefore, a wise intercessor will always seek to view the Enemy through the eyes of Jesus.

Jesus did His homework. He did not step into the arena of human existence without first surveying this Enemy-occupied territory. Satan's forces paraded across the earth asserting pride, deceit and rebellion. Determined to counter this exhibition, Jesus attired Himself in humility, truth and obedience. Philippians 2:6-8 describes it this way:

> Who, being in very nature God, did not consider equality with God something to be grasped, but made himself nothing, taking the very nature of a servant, being made in human likeness. And being found in appearance as a man, he humbled himself and became obedient to death—even death on a cross!

During His earthly ministry, Jesus exposed the work of the devil. The personal challenges of Satan were met head-on during the temptation in the wilderness.

Throughout His 33 years on earth, the Savior regularly disputed false beliefs, healed the sick and cast out demons. At every point of Enemy occupation, Jesus unmasked the perpetrators of hell. His final victory at Calvary totally "disarmed the powers and authorities" and "made a public spectacle of them" (Colossians 2:15).

Leaving a handful of men and women full of His Spirit, Jesus returned to His Father's side. This small band of believers continued to listen for His voice, follow His directions and proclaim the victory of Calvary. Within a short time, they had gained the reputation of turning the known world upside down (see Acts 17:6). Following their example, each generation of Christians has responded to the summons to meet with the Lord and view their commission through His eyes.

It isn't enough to simply know the facts and doctrines of our faith. An intercessor must be intimately acquainted with the Lord to view the world from His perspective. That requires a great deal of time walking and talking with Him, seeking His face in worship, and finding His heart on any matter. The consequence of acting outside His directives is always fruitlessness.

IDENTIFY THE ENEMY

Throughout this book, we have referred to the forces against which we war. Without giving undue importance to the enemy of our souls, it would be wise to gain a clear understanding of him and how he operates. The Bible provides a great amount of information concerning Satan and his followers so that we might view them from God's standpoint.

Originally, the Father, Son and Holy Spirit created Satan and his followers. Scripture indicates that they were part of the angelic host, with Satan being called *Lucifer*, meaning "morning star" (Isaiah 14:12). In Ezekiel 28:12-19, God describes Lucifer as follows:

"The model of perfection, full of wisdom and perfect in beauty. You were in Eden, the garden of God; every precious stone adorned you: ruby, topaz and emerald, chrysolite, onyx and jasper, sapphire, turquoise and beryl. Your settings and mountings were made of gold; on the day you were created they were prepared. You were anointed as a guardian cherub, for so I ordained you. You were on the holy mount of God; you walked among the fiery stones. You were blameless in your ways from the day you were created till wickedness was found in you. Through your widespread trade you were filled with violence, and you sinned. So I drove you in disgrace from the mount of God, and I expelled you, O guardian cherub, from among the fiery stones. Your heart became proud on account of your beauty, and you corrupted your wisdom because of your splendor. So I threw you to the earth; I made a spectacle of you before kings. By your many sins and dishonest trade you have desecrated your sanctuaries. So I made a fire come out from you, and it consumed you, and I reduced you to ashes on the ground in the sight of all who were watching. All the nations who knew you are appalled at you; you have come to a horrible end and will be no more."

Lucifer had been wise and beautiful. His place of anointing as a guardian cherub and one who walked among the fiery stones on the mount of God indicates great authority among the angelic host. But his splendor caused him to become prideful and his wisdom became corrupted.

Five times Lucifer exalted himself above our Lord with the words, "I will":

> For thou hast said in thine heart, *I will* ascend into heaven, *I will* exalt my throne above the stars of God: *I will* sit also upon the mount of the congregation, in the sides of the north: *I will* ascend above the heights of the clouds; *I will* be like the most High (Isaiah 14:13, 14, KJV, italics added).

The Trinity responded by casting Lucifer out of heaven. Jesus acknowledged this event when He said, "I saw Satan fall like lightning from heaven" (Luke 10:18). Taking up residence over Planet Earth, Lucifer became Satan, "the ruler of the kingdom of the air" (Ephesians 2:2) and "the god of this world" (2 Corinthians 4:4, KJV). These names testify to his lofty ambition of becoming master of the world.

Satan is a throne stealer. If he can't sit on God's throne in the heavens, he wants to sit enthroned on God's earthly royal seat. A replica of the heavenly throne mentioned in Isaiah 14, God's earthly throne is also called the "mount of the congregation" and is located "on the sides of the north." Psalm 48:1, 2 identifies this mountain as Mount Zion in Jerusalem: "Great is the Lord, and greatly to be praised in the city of our God, in the mountain of his holiness. Beautiful for situation, the joy of the whole earth, is mount Zion, on the sides of the north, the city of the great King" (KJV).

The Bible gives a panoramic picture of Satan's attempts to destroy God's chosen people and lay claim to this throne secured for Messiah. In Exodus 1:15-17, Satan used Pharaoh to order the destruction of all Jewish boy babies. However, the Jewish midwives defied the order and the babies lived. God responded in power as He rescued Moses and caused him to be raised in Pharaoh's court.

Later, the throne rights were given to the house of King David until the arrival of the Messiah (see 1 Chronicles 29:22, 23; Acts 2:30). In 2 Kings 11, Satan employed Queen Athaliah in an attempt to wipe out the royal family and therefore the royal line of David. Princess Jehosheba, however, stole young Prince Joash and hid him in the Temple. For six years, Joash lived undetected by the evil queen until Jehoiada the priest restored him to the throne. Neither did Satan suspect that God's provision existed so close at hand!

King Herod's murder of all the children in Bethlehem was another strategy of Satan to destroy Messiah Jesus (Matthew 2:16). Again, Satan failed; Jesus lived. Next, when he masterfully orchestrated the Crucifixion, the Prince of Darkness was sure he had finally annihilated the One destined for the royal throne. But his scheme became his eternal ruin when Jesus rose triumphant from the grave.

The usurper had been beaten. "Since the children have flesh and blood, he [Christ] too shared in their humanity so that by his death he might destroy him who holds the power of death—that is, the devil" (Hebrews 2:14). It was a man, Adam, who had originally sinned and surrendered his dominion of earth to Satan. It was the God-man, Jesus, who bought back the right of ruler-ship (Romans 5:12-21). Almighty God became the human heir to King David's throne (Luke 1:32; Acts 2:30). Jesus now held legal, spiritual and physical claim to the throne of the Lord.

Jesus commissioned His disciples as His royal ambas-sadors to take this news to the world. The authority and power He bestowed on them were a foretaste of the ruler-ship they would one day share with Him (2 Timothy 2:12; Revelation 5:10; 22:5). Jesus then returned to heaven to reign with His Father at the heavenly throne. Soon He will come again and enter Jerusalem to sit upon His earth-ly throne.

> Of the increase of his government and peace there shall be no end, upon the throne of David, and upon his kingdom, to order it, and to estab-lish it with judgment and with justice from henceforth even for ever. The zeal of the Lord of hosts will perform this (Isaiah 9:7, KJV).

> At that time they shall call Jerusalem the throne of the Lord; and all the nations shall be gathered unto it, to the name of the Lord, to Jerusalem: neither shall they walk any more after the imag-ination of their evil heart (Jeremiah 3:17, KJV).

One would think Satan's defeat would have settled the matter. This was true in the courts of heaven but not accepted in the camp of Satan. Even though Satan and his forces were disarmed, paraded before all heaven and heard the final judgment reserved for them, they are still in denial (see John 12:31, 32; John 16:11). Romans 1:21-32 states that those who turn their backs on God will be given a depraved mind and will believe a lie. Satan stands as one who has turned his back on God. Having already corrupted his wisdom, he now has a depraved mind and actually believes the lies he propagates. He doesn't accept his defeat at the cross; he still thinks he can rule heaven and earth!

In his quest for the Lord's throne in Jerusalem, Satan is determined to kill, steal and destroy both believers and unbelievers alike. His pattern of destruction continues. Throughout the 20th century, wars have increased in number and fatalities. During World War II, Satan used Hitler to destroy millions of Jews and Christians in the Holocaust. Divorce is currently at an all-time high. Suicide runs rampant among our teenagers. It is estimated that more Christians have died for their faith during the 20th century than in all the previous centuries combined. Jihad, a holy war of death, is still carried out by Muhammadans in some countries against Christians and others who oppose Islam.

It is no accident that the Middle East is a hotbed of war. The hostilities against Israel are in reality a spiritual war over a tiny bit of land that has great spiritual significance. Satan is determined to own Jerusalem. Currently, the Islamic Dome of the Rock in Jerusalem sits upon Mount Zion "on the sides of the north"— the location of the future earthly throne of the Lord. Satan intends that neither Jew nor Christian should have access to that site, as he holds it in reserve for the Antichrist.

Satan's *modus operandi* continues into the end times when he sets up his representative, the Antichrist, to be worshiped as God in the temple at Jerusalem. "He will oppose and will exalt himself over everything that is called God or is worshiped, so that he sets himself up in God's temple, proclaiming himself to be God" (2 Thessalonians 2:4). Verse 8 tells us that the Antichrist will be destroyed with the brightness of the Lord's second coming.

Finally, at the end of the Millennium, Satan is released for a short time from the pit where he has been confined. Keeping with his former pattern, he deceives the nations and gathers them for battle against Jerusalem. God's judgment is quick; fire consumes Satan's army. Satan reaps his final judgment: "And the devil that deceived them was cast into the lake of fire and brimstone, where the beast and the false prophet are, and shall be tormented day and night for ever and ever" (Revelation 20:10, KJV).

Throughout the centuries, Satan has been seeking the throne rights to people's hearts. Once he deceives a person, he pursues families, communities, nations and continents. Always looking to be worshiped and always looking to rule, his ultimate goal is to reign as God upon the Lord's throne in Jerusalem. He does not work alone but commands a devious army.

When Satan revolted, many "angels who did not keep their positions of authority but abandoned their own home" (Jude 6) chose to follow in his rebellion. These fallen angels came under the authority of Satan and are

now called demons. Note how the following phrases link
Satan as being in authority over the fallen angels:
"Beelzebub, the prince of demons" (Matthew 12:24);
"the devil and his angels" (Matthew 25:41); and "the
dragon and his angels" (Revelation 12:7, 9). According
to Jude 6, many of these demons are currently "kept in
darkness, bound with everlasting chains for judgment on
the great Day." Others are free and act as Satan's forces
in resisting the Lord's work.

Ephesians 6:12 provides a rough overview of the structure of these forces. "For our struggle is not against flesh
and blood, but against the rulers, against the authorities,
against the powers of this dark world and against the spiritual forces of evil in the heavenly realms."

- *Rulers*, (Greek, *archas*) means "masters or chief
  strategists." Many believe these high-ranking
  demons are assigned government systems and
  nations over which to rule. The prince of the
  Persian kingdom mentioned in Daniel 10:13
  may have been one such ruler.

- *Authorities* (Greek, *exousias*) denotes "powers."
  Demons of this level may be appointed against
  all persons in earthly authority such as government leaders, employers, heads of households
  and church leaders.

- *Powers of this dark world* (Greek, *kosmokratoras*)
  represents "world rulers." We might assume that
  these demons enforce darkness upon the world
  through the media, trends, customs and music.

Spiritual forces of evil (Greek, *pneumatika poner-ias*) indicates "demons assigned to the heaven-ly realm." Their mission may be to keep the church out of the presence of God through temptations and accusations. They are like the fowls of the air that steal the seed of the Word planted in men's hearts (Mark 4:4, 15).

Scripture also suggests that demons correlate their activities and that some are more depraved than others (see Matthew 12:43-45). But all evil spirits, regardless of rank, promote Satan's agenda and hinder the work of the Lord. Since Satan is not omnipresent, or everywhere at once, his army carries out his schemes across the earth.

Although demons are evil, they understand the deity and authority of Jesus because they once worshiped Him. The information collected over thousands of years con-cerning humans gives them an advantage over those believers who have only been here a short time. Having heard the judgment pronounced against them, they know it will someday be executed. Demons clearly comprehend the authority a believer wields when he uses the name of Jesus. Still, these forces of evil have a major denial prob-lem—unless forced to do so, they do not acknowledge the victory of Calvary. Through various tactics, they persist in attempting to exalt themselves over the Lord God.

KNOW YOUR ENEMY'S TACTICS

Satan regularly conducts reconnaissance work against both believers and unbelievers. He looks for weaknesses and possible inroads that his forces can use for infiltra-tion. As intercessors we need to be alert "in order that

Satan might not outwit us. For we are not unaware of his schemes" (2 Corinthians 2:11).

My husband often comments on how slow we are to detect the schemes of the devil. There are times our home has been in an upheaval with sickness, kids having nightmares and a heaviness that hangs in the air. These are combined with multiple people problems in the congregation. After struggling under these stresses, he will inevitably fix his tired eyes on mine and comment, "I think a demonic fireball has landed in our living room." For days we had lived with the "fireball" without recognizing it! Spiritual warfare halts the intrusion once we finally recognize we are under demonic attack.

Satan's tactics fall into three general categories. First, there are the flaming arrows of Ephesians 6:16. These demonic arrows often come as surprise attacks to people who are unaware that such things exist (Hosea 4:6). To us who know the Lord and His Word, these arrows can be identified and extinguished before they ever cause damage. But a lack of alertness can cause weakness in our defenses.

Flaming arrows come in a variety of styles and are used for different purposes. The following are just a few examples of specifically designed arrows aimed at strategic areas. Some sicknesses are arrows designed to destroy a person's body. Accusation is a flaming arrow aimed at a person's heart (Revelation 12:10), while lies and deception are directed at the level of a person's mind (John 8:44). The arrow of fear points toward a person's emotions (2 Timothy 1:7). The last three are successful only when the victims are unaware that their thoughts and feelings were the suggestion of a demon rather than from themselves or another person. Alert Christians will recognize such assaults and refuse to give them a place in their inner mind. They repulse such attacks by holding up their shield of faith.

Second, one may find strong resistance and hindrance to the work of the Lord. Paul referred to such roadblocks in 1 Thessalonians 2:18: "For we wanted to come to you—certainly I, Paul, did, again and again—but Satan stopped us." This was the same type of resistance that Daniel felt in his intercession. In chapter 4, we referred to Daniel's encounter with an angel as he stood by a riverbank. This incident occurred after Daniel had prayed and fasted for three weeks. Daniel 10:11-13 records the angel's explanation for the delay in responding to Daniel's intercession. For three weeks the angel had been resisted in delivering his message by a high-ranking demon called "the prince of the Persian kingdom." Finally, the archangel Michael intervened and the resistance was broken.

As in Daniel's experience, answers to prayer may be hindered by demons. One can experience spiritual roadblocks in the form of legal or physical opposition to the Lord's work. Severe weather conditions can impede missionary work and sometimes they are demon-related. Many Christians testify to the difficulties they experience before going on a missions trip or retreat. Delayed passports, lost luggage and unexpected hardships all point to demonic resistance. At times these hindrances succeed. One wonders if Paul's desire to visit the Thessalonians might have been fulfilled if there had been more intercessors praying for him.

The third tactic of our Enemy is temptation. If temptation succeeds, it provides Satan a doorway into people's lives. James 1:13-15 explains the downward progress of a successful temptation scheme:

> When tempted, no one should say, "God is tempting me." For God cannot be tempted by evil, nor does he tempt anyone; but each one is tempted when, by his own evil desire, he is dragged away and enticed. Then, after desire has conceived, it gives birth to sin; and sin, when it is full-grown, gives birth to death.

Note how a person's desire for the forbidden causes entrapment. Once sin is allowed to grow, it will eventually produce death. Temptation itself does not cause sin; giving into the temptation does. Jesus was tempted just as we are, but He never submitted to its lure. As a result He could say, "The prince of this world is coming. He has no hold on me" (John 14:30). Surrendering to temptation gives the Enemy a place . . . a doorway . . . for further torment.

Satan and his forces don't fight fair. Frequently they use all of the above strategies in their resistance to the finished work of Calvary. Their mission is to steal, kill and destroy by any means possible (John 10:10). Although they are not responsible for all sickness, they can cause blindness, injury, epilepsy, suicide, dumbness, insanity, and other various illnesses and deformities (see Matthew 12:22; Mark 9:17-27; Luke 8:26-37; 13:11-17). They are the power that stands behind idol worship (1 Corinthians 10:19-21). Within the church they encourage Christians to leave the faith, promote false teaching and advocate legalism (1 Timothy 4:1-3).

Their resistance, however, is shattered by those who know the power of the Cross and refuse to allow them to conduct their illegal activities. Those who fight the good fight of faith can stand in confidence and say with Paul, "For I know whom I have believed and I am convinced that He is able to guard what I have entrusted to Him until that day" (2 Timothy 1:12, *NASB*).

Application

1. Why is it important to view the forces of evil through the eyes of Jesus? How do intercessors continue to gain the Lord's perspective?

2. How does understanding the origin, objectives, and operating structure of Satan and his forces aid an intercessor?

3. The author spoke of three general tactics demonic forces use against people. From your personal experience, give an example of each. Why is it important for an intercessor to comprehend each of these strategies?

Chapter *10* Ten

Demonic Strongholds

*H*annah took deep breaths of freedom. Earlier she had come to me requesting deliverance. Her spirit guides had been tormenting her in the night and she did not know how to make them leave. After many questions her story tumbled out. As a teenager, Hannah had become involved with a board game that experimented with the occult. She and her friends had become so good at the game that they could play it in the spirit realm within the confines of their own bedrooms. Although miles apart from each other, they could cause damage to one another. Hannah had the physical scars of knife wounds inflicted on her from these game encounters. Her real game-mates turned out to be demonic spirits.

By the time Hannah realized this, she was caught in their web, unable to free herself. Deliverance was attained as each demonic spirit's curse was broken over Hannah through repentance. Their power and work of destruction were shattered by the authority of Jesus and His work at Calvary. Freedom for Hannah was sweet as the hidden activities of demons were exposed and destroyed.

GUERRILLA WARFARE

Satan and his forces operate in guerrilla warfare. Guerrillas are irregular military forces working illegally within a country or kingdom ruled by another. They operate out of bases established in hidden places. In the physical realm, guerrillas operate from places such as forests, mountains, jungles and even large cities. Examples would be the Vietcong during the Vietnam War, modern-day terrorists and the Mafia.

In the spiritual realm, demonic forces operate much the same way. They establish bases in places unseen by human eyes from which they launch their assaults. These places are usually hidden behind false religions or other environments of sin. Kathmandu, the capital city of Nepal, is full of temples dedicated to thousands of Hindu gods. Bangkok serves as a base of prostitution and child pornography. Anytime sin is allowed to reign in the physical world, a spiritual door will open for the establishment of demonic bases.

Guerrillas need assistance from the local population in order to operate. In the physical world, guerrillas depend on their support for food, shelter and information. They may also receive aid in the form of weapons and recruits. This assistance may be given willingly or under force. Likewise, Satan and his demons usually cannot operate without the aid of people who often unknowingly and unwillingly give them support. Kathmandu and Bangkok have populations that participate in false religions and activities of sexual sin. Both serve as examples of human support for demonic operations.

Demonic bases of operation also exist on the community level. You probably have noticed how some communities reflect a certain philosophy such as the New Age. Every bookstore and gift shop will carry New Age materials, and the restaurants will be decorated with crystals or other New Age objects. One town near us is known countywide as the hotbed of gang activity and violence. Another has the reputation of being a party town. At one time, the university in that area had to close down its annual week of open house because of excessive carousing and riots.

Proximity to these bases often results in spiritual attack (2 Peter 2:7, 8). Our oldest daughter opened a Christian coffeehouse next door to an adult bookstore. Demonic opposition from this pornography store caused confusion, anger and depression to settle over her at the coffeehouse. These traits were opposite to her cheerful, outgoing personality. Only intercession and a strong Christian stand carried her through those times.

Another example of spiritual attack comes from neighbors. Ty and Ronda asked us over one afternoon because their young son was having nightmares. The family had hardly slept in a week. Joining us were several friends from the church. Ty explained that his wife had been impressed by the Holy Spirit that the source of the problem lay somewhere in the cliff below their new home. A friend had also perceived the same thing during her prayer time. Separately, Ty had remembered a crude shelf built into the cliff that contained items he felt had been used for occult practices.

After praying together, the group developed a spiritual plan of action. Each couple was given a large stone on which they were to write a Scripture reference, such as Psalm 91. They were then to place the stone at one of the four corners of the property and, by prayer, establish the spiritual boundary lines of the property. We then met at the cliff, where the women interceded while the men descended. Reaching the crude shelf, they proceeded to dismantle it. After a half hour of intercession, sweat and avoiding poison oak, the work was completed. The nightmares ceased.

These same guerrilla forces operate on a personal level. Satan's forces will look for areas of weakness caused by individual sin to set up camp. These places may or may not be the choice of an individual. For example, a man who chooses to indulge in pornography opens himself up to demonic defilement. The child who is the victim of sexual abuse also becomes a victim of demonic violation. Sin allows a place from which Satan can torment both individuals.

STRONGHOLDS OF DARKNESS

Remember our diagram in chapter 5, describing the soul-filter? Areas where sin had penetrated our lives altered our perception of God, ourselves and the world around us. Our thoughts, feelings and ability to choose wisely were affected. These damaged, wounded areas became bases of operation where the Enemy could torment us. We called them strongholds.

The word *stronghold* can be understood two ways. It can reflect the strong hold or grip the Enemy has on us (or a family, community, nation, etc.). It can also be understood as a spirit fortress with high, massive walls that have become a base of operation for the forces of darkness. The walls of these fortresses rise above our view of Jesus and block the understanding of His Word (2 Corinthians 10:3-6). Christians who live with strongholds in their lives are hindered in their Christian growth. The unsaved live in blindness to the gospel caused by the overshadowing of various strongholds. In 2 Corinthians 4:2-6, the apostle Paul identifies several things that create strongholds—secret and shameful ways, deception, and distortion of God's Word. He also explains the blindness caused by the domination of satanic strongholds. Only the truth of Jesus Christ can dispel the darkness and bring clarity to people's minds.

The sins of secret and shameful ways, deception, and distortion of God's Word may be viewed as blueprints to numerous strongholds. As a master architect, Satan presents these blueprints to interested persons through various tactics. He and his demons then act as the builders of these fortresses. The resulting stronghold is owned, either by the person who commissioned the work or another. (Again, this would be the person choosing sin or the victim receiving the sin.) Any promoting of or participating in the building of these strongholds always results in bondage for the new owner (Isaiah 5:18). Unfortunately, the demonic builders don't leave after construction is completed. They stick around and act as if they own the place. They set up camp and use it as a base of operation from which they promote their evil work. Sometimes the

owner of the building is oblivious to their presence and
becomes a willing participant in their activities.

Many of these satanic blueprints include curses. We
can define a curse as a judgment stated against a person,
family, community or nation that acts as a beacon for
demonic activity. These beacons are like neon lights
over a stronghold that advertise the demonic activity
within the stronghold. Eventually the beacons must be
extinguished (broken) and the original blueprints
destroyed (sin renounced) in order for the existing
stronghold to be demolished.

Any sin that masters a person indicates a stronghold in
that person's life (2 Peter 2:19). The following examples
might be found in blueprints that could be obtained from
"Satan's Stronghold Builders, Inc."

SECRET AND SHAMEFUL WAYS

- All types of sexual sin—including homosexuality, bestiality and incest—result in defilement
  (Leviticus 18:6-24).

- Those who return evil for good invite evil to set
  up camp in their homes (Proverbs 17:13).

- Involvement in occult activity brings a curse
  (Leviticus 19:26, 31; 20:6; Deuteronomy 7:25,
  26; 13:1-5 18:9-14; Ephesians 5:11).

- Various expressions of rebellions will bring curses upon a person (Deuteronomy 27, 28; 1
  Samuel 15:23; Galations 3:13, 14).

- Curses can be transferred to succeeding generations or a willing recipient (Genesis 27:12, 13;

Deuteronomy 28:45, 46; Hosea 4:6; Matthew 27:24, 25.)

DECEPTION

- Believing that one doesn't have to forgive another creates demonic torment and a stronghold (Matthew 18:34, 35).

- Bitterness causes bondage and defiles others (Acts 8:23; Hebrews 12:15).

- Idol worship builds generational strongholds (Deuteronomy 5:9).

- Stubbornness, or refusing to release your personal false beliefs, is the same as idolatry (1 Samuel 15:23).

DISTORTION OF GOD'S WORD

- Envy, selfish ambition and strife distort God's truth and attract demonic forces (James 3:14-16).

- Preaching an untrue gospel brings a curse (Galatians 1:6-9).

- Prejudice against God's people and His promises for them brings curses (Genesis 12:3).

Strongholds can be built over physical areas. When authority figures make evil choices that affect those under their authority, a stronghold can result. For example, Hitler's choices brought all of Germany under a demonic stronghold during World War II. This is why 1 Timothy 2:1, 2 admonishes us to pray for those in authority.

In much the same way, a whole community may come

In much the same way, a whole community may come under the influence of demonic forces. When acts of violence are committed within that community or ungodly practices are encouraged, then the consequence may be a demonic stronghold. To counter these strongholds, Jeremiah 29:7 admonishes us to pray for the peace of our city. Earlier, I mentioned Ty and Ronda's experience of a family who came under the influence of a neighborhood stronghold. Intercessors can stop things before they happen or negate the spiritual repercussions after the event occurs.

Churches can experience strongholds. Demonic assignments will seek to influence the members of a fellowship. They gain permission to set up camp in the spirit over the congregation. Once a certain sin has been permitted to grow, it will eventually cause a spiritual deadness to overshadow the whole church. Sins of legalism and false teaching are only two examples (1 Timothy 4:1-3).

Not everything that confronts us is a stronghold. Many times we just "cross paths" with enemy troops out on reconnaissance. Encountering them does not verify a spiritual stronghold. Often we clash with another person's personality and we must be careful not to label such things as demonic. As people, we will always struggle with our flesh, or sin nature, even if we never have to deal with another demon! Only when a sin has mastered a person by dictating his or her reasoning or dominates a place, will we detect demonic strongholds. The command of Jesus to His first disciples is also His command to every intercessor: "Behold, I send you forth as sheep in the midst of wolves: be ye therefore wise as serpents, and harmless as doves" (Matthew 10:16, KJV).

1. Define spiritual strongholds and describe how they are built. What indicators would cause an intercessor to suspect the presence of a spiritual stronghold?

2. Sometimes intercessors mistake personality clashes or differences of opinion as signs of demonic activity. How can you tell the difference between what is demonic, what is flesh (sinful nature), and what is just another's viewpoint? What would be the proper way to deal with each?

Destroying Demonic Strongholds

*S*piritual warfare provides intercessors with the privilege of setting captives free and pillaging the works of the Enemy. What was intended for destruction and a trophy of evil can become plunder for the house of our God. No intercessor fights alone, because the Lord has committed Himself to battle against those who contend with us in spiritual warfare.

> Can plunder be taken from warriors, or captives rescued from the fierce? But this is what the Lord says: "Yes, captives will be taken from warriors, and plunder retrieved from the fierce; I will contend with those who contend with you, and your children I will save" (Isaiah 49:24, 25).

Some battles of contemporary warfare are fought and

won within a short period of time. Others involve a longer duration, as soldiers mount siege against an enemy fortification. Submarines and battleships are used during engagements at sea. Jet fighters are part of an aerial attack. Foot soldiers, tanks and missiles make up a ground assault. Jungle warfare is fought differently than desert warfare. No battle is the same, because different weapons and strategies define the distinctive features of each engagement.

So it is in spiritual warfare. Many battles are won during one session of prayer. Others require days and years of intercession. Jericho was taken with different strategies and weapons than when Joshua had fought the Amalekites at Rephidim (Joshua 5:13—6:21; Exodus 17:8-13). Though we may learn from past experiences, we must never expect the Holy Spirit to do things in exactly the same way again. Be open to learn from the past, but don't get locked into a formula.

There are, however, certain key elements found in every individual or territorial demonic stronghold. These elements are everything that opposes truth—deception, lies and wrong reasoning. Wrong reasoning and belief systems need to be recognized before they can be pulled down.

For though we walk in the flesh, we do not war according to the flesh, for the weapons of our warfare are not of the flesh, but divinely powerful for the destruction of fortresses. We are destroying speculations and every lofty thing raised up against the knowledge of God, and we are taking every thought captive to the obedience of Christ (2 Corinthians 10:3-5, NASB).

On an individual level, these strongholds can be identified by listening to someone's self-talk: "I don't have an anger problem—I'm just intense." "People don't like me." "I'm a free agent and can do what I want." These wrong reasonings create belief systems that dictate our actions and relationships. What begins in an individual can be magnified in a culture. Communism, Islam, gay pride and our culture's "victim mentality" are only a few examples.

The process of pulling down a demonic stronghold will vary according to the direction of the Holy Spirit. But two basic steps will be the same, because they are the avenue through which truth opposes darkness. Yet, how these steps are implemented will be original and creative.

STEP 1: REVOKING THE RIGHT OF THE ENEMY

"The Spirit of the Sovereign Lord is on me, because the Lord has anointed me to preach good news to the poor" (Isaiah 61:1). As Christians, we are on the offensive, not the defensive. The gates of hell cannot remain standing in any demonic stronghold when a prayer warrior comes against them in the anointing of Jesus Christ (Matthew 16:18). The gates of hell are Satan's headquarters where he conducts the government of his forces. When the Holy Spirit reveals the gates of hell in a stronghold, the intercessor has a key to its destruction. The sin that gave Satan the right to construct and operate a stronghold is revoked and the gates destroyed. The stronghold is overtaken and demolished.

The right of the Enemy to operate a stronghold can be revoked through the confession, repentance, and forsaking of the sin or of the untruth that originally gave darkness a place to enter (Proverbs 28:13; James 5:16; 1 John

1:8-10). The sin is identified and confessed as a sin committed by or against the individual. For those who committed the sin, repentance must be announced and the sin forsaken. For those who are the victims of sin, then the act of repentance is relinquishing their right to hold onto the pain of the sin. This is done by forgiving the offender and releasing the sin to the Lord. Jesus must be given ownership of that for which He died—in this case, the horrible sin done against the person.

On an individual level, repentance must come from the person caught in the stronghold. In some cases, repentance can be sought by someone who will stand in proxy for the person (as when a generational stronghold needs to be broken by a descendant of the person or persons who first opened the door to the Enemy). On a broader level, such as a community or nation, repentance can be sought by representatives of that community or nation:

> If my people, who are called by my name, will humble themselves and pray and seek my face and turn from their wicked ways, then will I hear from heaven and will forgive their sin and will heal their land. Now my eyes will be open and my ears attentive to the prayers offered in this place (2 Chronicles 7:14, 15).

Another way to revoke the right of the Enemy is to apply a promise of God to the situation. This is like serving a legal injunction against Satan and his forces. They must comply with the law established at Calvary. The promises of God give the intercessor constitutional rights of the new covenant that the Enemy must acknowledge and obey.

An example of this would be the intercession a mother makes for her son who has embraced the sin of homosexuality. The son may have no intention of repenting, yet the promises of God give the mother authority to revoke the Enemy's deception of her son. Two promises she might claim are these:

> Believe in the Lord Jesus, and you will be saved—you and your household (Acts 16:31).

> I will say to the north, "Give them up!" and to the south, "Do not hold them back." Bring my sons from afar and my daughters from the ends of the earth—everyone who is called by my name, whom I created for my glory, whom I formed and made (Isaiah 43:6, 7).

In supplication, the mother stands before the throne of God and pleads for her son by using these promises. She then presents them to Satan in spiritual warfare as a legal injunction against his work of deception. The mother then has a clear path in prayer to pull down the wrong reasonings and arguments which have deceived her son.

This same principle works on a community and national level. The promises of God apply to individuals and to the culture in which individuals live. Isaiah 26:2 stands as one of the hallmark promises declaring that the forces of darkness must open their gates to the kingdom of God: "Open the gates that the righteous nation may enter, the nation that keeps faith." Isaiah 55:5-7 and 65:1-9 may also be used as court orders against the spiritual forces that blind nations to the freedom of Jesus Christ.

Sometimes both methods will be needed. Much of the activity of spiritual warfare takes place during this first step. This is where the beacons of a stronghold (its curses) are broken and its gates are kicked in so that freedom may be accomplished. This may take time because the forces of darkness resist those who enforce Calvary's victory.

STEP 2: PROCLAIMING FREEDOM

"He has sent me to bind up the brokenhearted, to proclaim freedom for the captives and release from darkness for the prisoners, to proclaim the year of the Lord's favor and the day of vengeance of our God" (Isaiah 61:1, 2). The second step in breaking demonic strongholds is a proclamation of freedom, stated before principalities and powers and before those held as prisoners in strongholds. The stronghold has been entered; now its destruction can begin and its prisoners released.

The right to deceive has been revoked in step one. The intercessor now goes in and pulls down each brick of wrong reasoning and argument that the Enemy has constructed to block the knowledge of God. Pulling down these speculations and thinking patterns takes place in the spirit, but the results are seen in the physical. Those who have been held captive begin to see and understand truth. Clarity comes where once there was confusion and deception. This second step of proclamation takes many forms, depending on the leading of the Holy Spirit.

Only the truth found in Jesus Christ dispels darkness

and brings freedom. The basis of all legal advances against Satan's strongholds is Calvary. The armor of God, weapons and strategies of intercession originate from Calvary's cross. Each represents different aspects of truth against untruth, but all are used to destroy demonic strongholds. They will be explained in the chapters that follow.

ERECTING "NO TRESPASSING SIGNS"

Once a fortress of darkness has been annihilated, it must be declared "off limits" to future activity of the Enemy. This is accomplished by erecting "no trespassing signs" in the spirit realm. Scriptures used to destroy strongholds are spiritual signposts of the victory of the Lord. They stand as reminders to demons that this place is no longer accessible to them. What had been a possession of the Enemy is now under the rulership of the Lord of Hosts.

These "no trespassing signs" can be referenced whenever the forces of darkness step over the boundaries of the newly acquired territory. Many intercessors record them in their intercession journals, along with a summary of how God led them in destroying a particular stronghold. Such a journal also serves as a reference to the Enemy if he threatens an area that he has vacated.

BUILDING STRONGHOLDS OF GODLINESS

The destruction of a demonic stronghold is only part of the work of an intercessor. Once the destruction is completed, the intercessor should "repair and make new" the old waste places. These waste places are the desolate ruins left behind after demonic activity has ceased or sin has been renounced. Turning waste places into beautiful habitations of the Spirit is necessary whenever individual or territorial devastation has occurred. Prayer begins the building process for a stronghold of godliness where a fortress of evil once stood.

> They will rebuild the ancient ruins and restore the places long devastated; they will renew the ruined cities that have been devastated for generations (Isaiah 61:4).

> Your people will rebuild the ancient ruins and will raise up the age-old foundations; you will be called Repairer of Broken Walls, Restorer of Streets with Dwellings (Isaiah 58:12).

Much of this process takes place before the throne in supplication. Strongholds of godliness are constructed as an intercessor beseeches God.

> To bestow on them [those set free] a crown of beauty instead of ashes, the oil of gladness instead of mourning, and a garment of praise instead of a spirit of despair. They will be called oaks of righteousness, a planting of the Lord for the display of his splendor (Isaiah 61:3).

The Holy Spirit will give a direction for prayer as each part of a stronghold of godliness is constructed.

In addition to prayer, disciplines such as renewing
the mind and walking in the power of the Holy Spirit
help rebuild individual waste places with strongholds of
holiness. Godly territorial strongholds are established
through deeds and activities that establish righteousness.

SPIRITUAL ALLIES

We are not alone in destroying demonic strongholds.
The Lord has assigned spiritual allies to help perform this
task. Angels (or "messengers" in the Greek or Hebrew)
encamp about each intercessor and aid in the work of
deliverance (Psalm 34:7; Daniel 6:22). These emissaries
carry out the Word of God when it is spoken forth under
the prompting of the Holy Spirit (Psalm 103:20). They
chase and persecute the retreating forces of darkness
(Psalm 35:5, 6).

Protection and service are also part of the angels' ministry
to an intercessor (Psalm 91:11, 12; Hebrews 1:14). All
of their activities on our behalf are directed by the Lord,
because we have not been given permission to pray to
angels. Everything that we need as intercessors is provided by the Holy Spirit, including the work of these
wonderful allies.

We may or may not see the work of angels as we intercede. Sometimes their activities are revealed to us so that
we might be encouraged. Elisha prayed that his servant
would have his spiritual eyes opened to the company of
angels that encircled them (2 Kings 6:15-17). Paul encouraged the sailors during a life-threatening storm with the
message he received from an angel (Acts 27:22-24). In
Genesis 31:1, 2, Jacob encountered a host of angels as he

and his family were returning home for a family reunion. Their encounter led him to call the name of the place *Mahanaim*, meaning "two camps, or two bands." A team of intercessors never encamps alone. A host of angels encamps alongside them to aid in their work.

During one session of prayer, an intercessor observed a host of angels encamped alongside her. As she began to pray, the angels rose from their positions of rest and picked up their swords and shields. Rising as a mighty army, the angels then went and stood over the different homes of church members in the community for which she was praying. A common standard was lifted over each home, and the intercessor knew that this banner represented the church she attended. Swords were wielded as freedom was declared over these homes where oppression resided. Her work and that of the angelic host were combined to usher in a new release of God's work.

There are other allies that enter into conflict against the enemies of God. The Scripture indicates that even the stars, earth, animals and the whole universe are in alliance with us against Satan and his demons (Judges 5:19-21; Numbers 22:26-33; Joshua 10:12). The earth is groaning and travailing as in birth, waiting for the return of Jesus Christ. Creation longs for the redemption that will be manifested when all Christians will be put on display and the new heavens and earth formed (Romans 8:19-22).

A Word of Caution

After the victory in Europe at the end of World War II, the allies were sickened to discover the atrocities committed against Jews, Poles and other Europeans. The liberation of the Nazi death camps revealed millions of people who had been murdered and dehumanized. When the liberators approached the concentration camps, what began as cries of victory became hushed silence, as they faced the stark realities of Hitler's strongholds of death. The details of horror from which these people were being set free would forever haunt their rescuers. Accounts of these horrors have been made known to the world in hopes they would never happen again. Hence, the purpose for studying the Holocaust is to scare us into realizing that unrestrained evil must be resisted. We do not reflect on these accounts to learn the proper techniques of warfare. They are exposed only as reasons for war, not as methods of warfare.

Demonic strongholds can be ugly. As you study intercession, be careful that you do not over-investigate the things of darkness. Some people want their flesh tingled by hearing horror stories of the work of the Enemy. Hearing the gross details of evil is not a healthy activity. The horrors of war are not trumpeted by returning veterans. Everything you need to know about spiritual warfare has been given in the Word of God and will be revealed by His Spirit. Experience in intercession will expose you to the filth of the Enemy; don't go looking for it. Deal with it when you encounter it, but don't study it.

Application

1. What are the key elements found in every demonic stronghold that must be recognized before a stronghold can be demolished? Give examples of these elements from past demonic strongholds you have encountered.

2. What are the two steps necessary in demolishing a demonic stronghold? How have you observed these steps carried out in spiritual warfare?

3. What necessary actions are required after a demonic stronghold is overtaken? Why are these important?

4. Angels are a popular topic in today's world. What unscriptural teaching have you heard concerning angels? What does Scripture teach about these ministering spirits?

Chapter *12* Twelve

The Garments of an Intercessor

*B*eneath the Cross the ground was covered with tents. Intercessors moved within the camp coming from their latest assignments. Angels walked among them unseen, yet their presence was perceived. Worship and praise could be heard throughout the encampment as intercessors prepared for the morning's activities. Some sat outside their tents inspecting and shining their armor. Several had already suited up and were gathering in groups ready to meet with their Lord. Dressed in their uniforms, these people of prayer radiated the glory of Calvary and glistened with the anointing of the Son.

Many spiritual garments are mentioned in the Bible, such as the garment of salvation, the robe of righteousness and the garment of praise. All are worn

167

by an intercessor. However, there is one suit of clothing given to each believer to which an intercessor pays particular attention, whether moving as a supplicant, warrior or watchman.

The uniform is called *the armor of God*. It is designed and provided free of charge by the Commander in Chief, Jesus Christ. It is essential attire for those who would fight against things they cannot see or often understand. Unfortunately, many intercessors leave their armor hanging in their prayer closet instead of wearing it! The responsibility of putting on our armor is ours alone; no one will do it for us.

> Put on the full armor of God so that you can take your stand against the devil's schemes. For our struggle is not against flesh and blood, but against the rulers, against the authorities, against the powers of this dark world and against the spiritual forces of evil in the heavenly realms. Therefore put on the full armor of God, so that when the day of evil comes, you may be able to stand your ground, and after you have done everything, to stand (Ephesians 6:11-13).

> The night is nearly over; the day is almost here. So let us put aside the deeds of darkness and put on the armor of light (Romans 13:12).

Each piece of armor interrelates with the others, because the effectiveness of the suit depends on each piece being properly worn. The neglect of even one piece can result in an ill-fitting suit and endanger the intercessor.

Worn together, the pieces reflect the victory won for us at Calvary.

The armor, however, provides no protection for the back of a warrior, because God intends for us to face our Enemy. We jeopardize our mission when we turn our back to the Evil One. And the Lord has promised to be our rear guard when we are in a warfare stance (Isaiah 52:12; 58:8).

Ephesians 6:14-17 describes the armor which God has provided for an intercessor:

> Stand firm then, with the belt of truth buckled around your waist, with the breastplate of righteousness in place, and with your feet fitted with the readiness that comes from the gospel of peace. In addition to all this, take up the shield of faith, with which you can extinguish all the flaming arrows of the evil one. Take the helmet of salvation and the sword of the Spirit, which is the word of God.

THE TUNIC

A simple tunic is worn under the armor of an intercessor. This tunic represents the unadorned garment of humility worn by Jesus throughout His ministry. Worn constantly, it keeps the armor from chafing the skin and allows a comfortable fit. The armor never fits properly if worn over a tunic of pride where the sweat of battle carries a stench and the armor becomes burdensome. Humility allows the sweat of battle to evaporate and cushions the weight of the armor. Its coarseness keeps a warrior from presumption, which is not uncommon even among seasoned intercessors. The tunic of humility stands in direct contrast to the glittering garments of a prideful enemy.

BELT OF TRUTH

Truth is the first piece of armor that an intercessor puts on over the tunic, because it is the foundation piece for the breastplate and sword. The proper placement of these two pieces of armor depends on a secure fit of the belt of truth. Too many warriors are ineffective in spiritual warfare because they excuse themselves from personal integrity. Truthfulness is defined by their own standards of honesty. The Father of Lies does not hesitate to take advantage of this flaw. He can see a breastplate and sword that have no firm attachment to a warrior. Intercessors must place the belt of truth around their waists and buckle the two sides tightly together.

The first side represents God's instructions, explained in Scripture, on how to walk rightly. His Word is the blueprint for personal integrity in all parts of our lives. This side of the belt of truth eliminates the danger of setting up our own gauge of right and wrong. The second side to the belt of truth has to do with walking out the instructions of integrity in our relationships. Little white lies, half-truths and misrepresentations are not allowed in the life of a warrior. Honesty before God and others must be tied together with an understanding of God's eternal Word in order to provide a secure support for additional armor. Daily we must put on our belt of truth by forsaking personal falsehoods and embracing the instructions of Scripture.

BREASTPLATE OF RIGHTEOUSNESS

The breastplate is composed of God's righteousness. We do not face the forces of evil attired in our own righteousness because we have none. Intercessors often feel unworthy, unwelcome or unusable by God, but that's the whole point of the gospel! We are people who are wrong—sinful, unusable and hopeless—until the *rightness* of Jesus covers our *wrongness* through His redemptive work at Calvary. It is His righteousness alone that protects the vital organs of our inner person.

Satan knows everything you have done wrong, and he'll parade your imperfections before you. He usually does this when you are getting too close for comfort, and he senses that you are a threat to his plans. God has provided His righteousness for you to wear, because your Enemy can find no fault in Christ Jesus. Without the breastplate of righteousness, an intercessor becomes an uncovered target for the penetration of demonic arrows.

As intercessors we put on the breastplate of righteousness by reminding ourselves and the devil that our *rightness* does not come from ourselves. Because of Jesus Christ and His shed blood, we stand before God with our sins—past, present and future—covered by that blood. Though we may acknowledge our past sins, they no longer are a part of us. They were severed at the

Cross. The power of His blood in our life overcomes our accuser. Revelation 12:10, 11 states it this way:

> Then I heard a loud voice in heaven say: "Now have come the salvation and the power and the kingdom of our God, and the authority of his Christ. For the accuser of our brothers, who accuses them before our God day and night, has been hurled down. They overcame him by the blood of the Lamb and by the word of their testimony; they did not love their lives so much as to shrink from death."

SHOES OF PEACE

At my house, we take off our shoes when we come in the front door. When the kids see me putting on my shoes, they ask, "Where are you going?" They know Mom may be headed someplace interesting and they want to be included. When intercessors put on their shoes of peace, it shows they are ready to go someplace. These particular shoes announce our intention of taking the gospel message to others through prayer.

Carrying that message won't be easy because the Enemy sets ambushes along the way. These shoes are designed for fighting the demonic forces that blind people to the message of the gospel of peace. Their construction allows prayer warriors to tread lightly when needed, but they also provide a firm stance to stand and fight. Intercessors wear footwear tailored to their particular feet by their own experience with the gospel. Dressed for war, their mission is one of peace.

Intercessors prepare their feet daily by reviewing their commission to declare the gospel message. They set themselves to war in the spirit while walking in peace among men. Prayer warriors whose shoes of peace are properly fitted see captives set free, according to the command of 2 Timothy 2:23-26:

> Don't have anything to do with foolish and stupid arguments, because you know they produce quarrels. And the Lord's servant must not quarrel; instead, he must be kind to everyone, able to teach, not resentful. Those who oppose him he must gently instruct, in the hope that God will grant them repentance leading them to a knowledge of the truth, and that they will come to their senses and escape from the trap of the devil, who has taken them captive to do his will.

·SHIELD OF FAITH

Faith is the name embossed on the shield of an intercessor. Hebrews 11:1 describes the shield's covering material as "the substance of things hoped for" and its frame as "the evidence of things not seen" (KJV). Its construction is light enough to be moved to various positions as needed to intercept flaming arrows, yet strong enough to stop such arrows. The translucent nature of the shield allows warriors to observe an incoming arrow without endangering themselves. Many warriors have been burned by examining a flaming dart too closely without their shield of faith! Experienced intercessors know that mastering a grip on such a shield takes time and practice.

A prayer warrior learns to position the shield of faith according to the promises of God. For example, an arrow of rejection is defused as the warrior holds the shield in the position of Ephesians 1:6: "Wherein he hath made us accepted in the beloved" (KJV). The various battle placements for the shield are learned by studying the Scriptures, because "faith cometh by hearing, and hearing by the word of God" (Romans 10:17, KJV).

Team and corporate intercessors have the added advantage of combining their shields for a protective covering during battle. Like Roman soldiers of old, they can cluster together with the middle warriors holding their shields above their heads and with those on the rim placing their shields outward. This forms protection like a turtle's shell that allows the team to advance unharmed to the base of an enemy stronghold where they can storm its walls.

As intercessors we daily take up our shield by viewing a situation through the eyes of faith. We must choose to trust in the Lord and refuse to allow fear or doubt to dictate our response to circumstances. Furthermore, our study in the Scriptures will equip us to instinctively position our shield against Satan's darts. Again, using our shield effectively takes time and practice!

HELMET OF SALVATION

Woe to the soldier who cannot think or direct the rest of his body in effective warfare because of a head wound. Woe to the soldiers who cannot be effective prayer warriors because they are wounded in the foundation of their beliefs—their understanding of salvation and the work of Jesus at Calvary!

Satan attempts to undermine our faith in Jesus Christ as personal Savior, because it is the only requirement for salvation. He will insist that you aren't good enough to be saved, or that you need to perform good works to ensure your salvation. (Good works are an outgrowth of salvation, not its origin.) Once your focus is off Jesus, your warfare becomes ineffective. You are no longer a threat to him!

A wise intercessor first fastens on the helmet of salvation, which is designed to stop all demonic attacks that would lie to your mind concerning the finished work of the Cross. Doubt is rejected by one whose helmet fits securely. We put on our helmet by reviewing scriptures such as John 3:16; Romans 3:22-26; 10:9, 10; and 1 John 5:20. Our confidence comes from knowing this fact: "It is by grace you have been saved, through faith—and this not from yourselves, it is the gift of God—not by works, so that no one can boast" (Ephesians 2:8, 9).

SWORD OF THE SPIRIT

Ephesians 6:17 identifies the sword of the Spirit as the Word of God: "Take . . . the sword of the Spirit, which is the word of God." It is the fundamental weapon of a prayer warrior. Burning as fire, it is able to shatter even the strongest fortress of the enemy: " 'Is not my word like fire,' declares the Lord, 'and like a hammer that breaks a rock in pieces?' " (Jeremiah 23:29).

A clear understanding of Scripture enables intercessors

to efficiently wage war. Although various weapons will be examined in subsequent chapters, they really are just different expressions of the sword of the Spirit.

The Greek language gives insights on this sword called the Word of God. *Logos* is used to refer to the Word of God you study, meditate on and place deep within your spirit. It is the combined scriptures of the Bible. I have heard it compared to the sheath or sword holder on the belt of a prayer warrior. When that *logos* becomes life within you, it is then a weapon for the Holy Spirit to use; it becomes *rhema*. *Rhema* means "utterance," and it is the word spoken in season that cuts through darkness and destroys the Enemy. During intercession, we bring a specific scripture (*rhema*) out of the whole Bible (*Logos*) for a specific purpose at a specific time.

I have a friend whom I avoid when it comes to prayer. No matter what the problem, she will rattle off scripture after scripture. If someone is sick, we hear her pray every healing verse in the Bible. If another is depressed, she will recite scriptures on joy. She throws every verse she can think of at God and at the devil. After 20 years she still acts like the novice who wildly swings both sword and sheath at anything that moves! Although the Word of God never returns void, the intercessor using the Word must use wisdom and be directed by the Holy Spirit.

Many times the Holy Spirit may want to emphasize a root cause of illness, such as unforgiveness. Another time He may want the prayer team to attack depression by surrounding the person and singing songs of deliverance (Psalm 32:7). An effective weapon will always reflect some aspect of Scripture and be directed by the Holy Spirit. Remember—He's in charge and it's His sword!

A sword is to no avail unless you know how to use it. Maturity in an intercessor comes from using and experiencing God's Word, not just knowing it. "Solid food is for the mature, who by constant use [of God's Word] have trained themselves to distinguish good from evil" (Hebrews 5:14).

We learn to use the sword of the Spirit in combat by praying His promises. It is through these promises that we are able to participate in the divine nature and escape the corruption found in the world (2 Peter 1:4). Likewise, our mission includes rescuing those caught in the corruption of the world. When the Holy Spirit brings a promise from Scripture to the attention of an intercessor, the Lord desires to see that promise become reality in the life of the person for whom the intercessor is interceding.

Years ago I was interceding for our oldest son, who was about to leave for a Discipleship Training School with Youth With a Mission. David loved the Lord but was at that age when he was trying to find his own identity and purpose in life. Caught up in my concerns, I was interrupted in my travail by a booming voice behind me saying, "I will." I immediately knew the Lord was both promising me those things for which I prayed and correcting me in my lack of trust in Him concerning my son. The scripture that came to me after this voice was Isaiah 46:8-11:

> "Remember this, fix it in mind, take it to heart, you rebels. Remember the former things, those of long ago; I am God, and there is no other; I am God,

and there is none like me. I make known the end
from the beginning, from ancient times, what is
still to come. I say: My purpose will stand, and I
will do all that I please. From the east I summon
a bird of prey; from a far-off land, a man to fulfill
my purpose. What I have said, that will I bring
about; what I have planned, that will I do."

For the next three months, this became my sword as
I continued to intercede. God was requiring me to
"remember the former things, those of long ago"—my
teen years and how He drew me close to Himself. He
was God then, and He would be so with my son now.
His purpose for David would be fulfilled. I knew the
"bird of prey" represented the removal of things in
David's life that stood between him and the Lord. I
envisioned the "man from a far-off land" to be an older
gentleman from another country who would influence
David in the ways of God. The Holy Spirit was up to
something, and I was able to participate in those plans
through prayer.

During those three months, we knew this promise
was being fulfilled in David. His phone calls indicated
that things were being removed from his life and that he
was growing in his relationship with the Lord. He spoke
highly of Matias, his team leader, who was from
Germany. I knew this must be the man from a far-off
land referred to in Isaiah 46.

That December, David's team had a few days' layover
in Los Angeles before they flew to Costa Rica for mission
work. We were able to visit with our son for several
hours. It was an exciting time for David because we got

to meet Matias, the man from a far country. Imagine my surprise when Matias turned out to be a long-haired, tattooed, 22-year-old firecracker of a Christian! He was not the distinguished gentleman I had pictured, but he was the man God had promised me for David. Thank goodness our ways are not His ways!

Every spiritual warrior finishes dressing for battle by taking up the sword of the Spirit. They know God's commission to Jeremiah has become their commission:

> Then the Lord reached out his hand and touched my mouth and said to me, "Now, I have put my words in your mouth. See, today I appoint you over nations and kingdoms to uproot and tear down, to destroy and overthrow, to build and to plant" (Jeremiah 1:9, 10).

Suit Up!

Many intercessors have worn their armor for so long it has become their second skin. Others are not aware that a piece of armor is missing until they find a flaming dart protruding from their side! I know of one intercession team who never addressed their prayer assignments because time was always consumed in reassuring the various team members of their salvation and usefulness. It never occurred to them that these warriors were neglecting to put on their helmet of salvation and breastplate of righteousness before coming to intercession. They had not been trained how to properly wear their armor.

It is not uncommon for intercessors to experience feelings of inadequacy, irritability or doubt before a time of prayer. If the Enemy knows we are going to prayer, he will throw all these things at us and we will feel them coming! Expect it. This happens to individual intercessors, team members, leaders of prayer warriors and leaders of leaders. None are exempt from these flaming flurries.

Yet, we can stand fully dressed, not influenced by these feelings. They can be intercepted and extinguished before affecting intercession. The breastplate of righteousness refuses inadequacy. The shoes of peace are not moved by irritability. Doubt is extinguished by the shield of faith.

Think about it . . . as committed intercessors, we cannot dwell on anything that opposes the armor of God. Do we think Jesus would throw these darts at us just to see if we are wearing our armor? I don't think so! We can identify these thoughts as attacks from the Enemy and refuse to allow them to influence our emotions and self talk. If we need confirmation about what we are feeling for intercession, we can talk to someone in authority or with other team members. They can establish the direction of the Holy Spirit and clairfy what might be darts of the Enemy or static from our soul. But first and foremost, let's grab our armor and suit up!

Intercessors who have been trained in how to wear and war in their spiritual armor will find private intercession effective. They will also be an asset on any prayer team. Study the different pieces of your armor and how they are used. Watch for signs in other team members to assure they have not forgotten a piece of their armor or may not be using the armor properly. When necessary, pull that flaming dart out and learn from the experience! As a team, practice forming shields of faith into a turtle and plan together how to lay siege to Enemy strongholds. Let none of us become casualties of war simply because we did not take the armor of God seriously! It truly is adequate for anything we may face in intercession.

Application

1. Give a short description of each piece of the armor of God, explaining why it is important and how to wear or use it.

2. What would be the indications that a particular piece of armor is missing from your uniform?

3. Give an example for each missing piece.

The Legal Library and Arsenal of an Intercessor—1

There are several women in our church who join me in prayer for important matters. Some of our church intercession teams are led by these women, and they have quite a reputation for answered prayer. Are these intercessors more special to God than the rest of us? No, the Lord loves us all the same. Are they more gifted in the ministry of intercession than the rest of us? Perhaps, but spiritual gifts do not validate a person's ministry or give extra influence with God or man. Is it because some are older and have years of experience? No. Many older people are not as effective at intercession, even though they have been intercessors for years.

What sets these people apart is their understanding of God's Word as the basis for intercession. Not only do they rely on Scripture, but they also adjust their attitudes and actions according to its directives. This gives them influence in the courts of heaven, on the battlefield and with those in need. This influence is available to anyone who becomes immersed in the Word of God . . . believes His principles . . . obeys His instructions. Scripture stands as a legal library for those involved in supplication, and a powerful arsenal for those involved as prayer warriors.

OUR LEGAL LIBRARY

My father is an attorney. His office is lined with legal books and documents of law used to form the basis of petitions in a court of law. They provide the legal grounds for any case he argues before a judge. Dad also needs to have correct and current facts to substantiate the legal claims of those he represents. How well he knows the law, plus the facts of the case, determines how successful he is in influencing the judge and jury to grant his requests. Likewise, the Word of God stands as the legal library for us.

The law for a supplicant is the new covenant established by Jesus Christ at Calvary. The old covenant, or the law of Moses, stands as a reference point for the new covenant, because it was Jesus who fulfilled all the old covenant (Matthew 5:17). In Him we stand before the Father as ones who have satisfied all the legal conditions required under the old law (Colossians 2:10-14). The New Testament (the *new covenant*), contains a record of these facts. Supplicants need a working understanding of the new covenant as they prepare their petitions for the court of heaven.

New intercessors will find that the Gospels and the Books of Romans and Hebrews contain many scriptures relating to the new covenant. The promises of God recorded in both the New and Old Testaments provide the intercessor with ultimate, irrefutable and constitutional rights. The stories contained throughout the Bible provide case histories to substantiate a petition before the throne. They illustrate the promises of God and act as precedents justifying what has been proven in past cases. These documents of the court of heaven are available for any supplicant to study.

An intercessor may have to do additional research to discover current and correct facts concerning a situation needing prayer. To intercede without correct information misdirects the petition. Gathering facts includes the interviewing of those involved in the situation. Since personal opinions are often tainted, it is wise to only ask for necessary facts. Separate opinions from facts and let the Holy Spirit provide guidance for your approach to intercession.

Intercessors praying for a community or nation should research the past as well as the current conditions of that area. The more information intercessors have, the more direct will be their intercession. This information can then be combined with the Word of God to help form their supplication. The more that Scripture is stored within the spirit of an intercessor, the easier it is for the Holy Spirit to draw upon this legal library. Even seasoned intercessors must go to prayer with their well-worn Bible open along with handwritten notes of the facts needing to be addressed.

God already knows the law and the facts concerning our petitions. Yet, He wants to dialogue with us about them: "Come now, and let us reason together, saith the Lord: though your sins be as scarlet, they shall be as white as snow; though they be red like crimson, they shall be as wool" (Isaiah 1:18, KJV). The Lord encourages us to review, argue and state the case for our intercession:

> I, even I, am he who blots out your transgressions, for my own sake, and remembers your sins no more. Review the past for me, let us argue the matter together; state the case for your innocence (Isaiah 43:25, 26).

After discussing a prayer need with the Holy Spirit and getting His directives, a supplicant approaches the Father with a summary of the petition. This is a time of presenting the "facts of the case." The intercessor then recites several Scriptural promises concerning the petition, reminding the Lord of how He has fulfilled these promises in the past. Finally, the intercessor might conclude the presentation with Scripture referring to the finished work of Jesus on Calvary. All the requests of intercession rest on His redemptive work. All of this might be intertwined with times of deep intercession called travail, times of praise, worship, dance or times of silence.

A POWERFUL ARSENAL

A prayer warrior uses Scripture in much the same way as a supplicant. The Word of God, as the sword of the Spirit, stands as the arsenal of all spiritual warfare. A modern-day soldier may use guns, tanks, missiles, battleships or aircraft. The Holy Spirit issues weapons and ammunition to intercessors as needed for the type of battle they face. Sometimes these may be as simple as a "Holy Spirit grenade." Other times we might be issued a "spiritual missile." The weapons vary, but they all reflect some aspect of the sword of the Spirit.

Whatever weapon is issued to us by the Holy Spirit is meant to be used! It becomes effective only when it becomes part of our intercession. A prayer warrior then becomes the Lord's greatest weapon against the forces of darkness: "You are my war club, my weapon for battle—with you I shatter nations, with you I destroy kingdoms, with you I shatter horse and rider, with you I shatter chariot and driver" (Jeremiah 51:20, 21).

None of these weapons will seem logical to the natural mind. They seem foolish. However, they are not designed for the natural but for the spiritual realm. Originating from the Holy Spirit, they attack those things that blind the minds of people. They are designed to pull down and destroy spiritual strongholds. They are specifically aimed at reasonings, imaginations and motives that have risen against the knowledge of God in people's minds.

Representing truth against deception, these weapons render powerless those demons who hold people captive to lies. Paul states it like this:

> For though we live in the world, we do not wage war as the world does. The weapons we fight with are not the weapons of the world. On the contrary, they have divine power to demolish strongholds. We demolish arguments and every pretension that sets itself up against the knowledge of God, and we

take captive every thought to make it obedient to
Christ (2 Corinthians 10:3-5).

King Joash was instructed by Elisha to do some very
odd things to secure the outcome of a war. These absurd
actions had great bearing on the spiritual realm. King
Joash, however, did not understand the spiritual importance of what the prophet was asking him to do. He won
a few battles, but his failure to grasp the implications of
spiritual warfare cost him the war.

> Elisha said, "Get a bow and some arrows," and he
> did so. "Take the bow in your hands," he said to
> the king of Israel. When he had taken it, Elisha put
> his hands on the king's hands.
>
> "Open the east window," he said, and he opened
> it. "Shoot!" Elisha said, and he shot. "The Lord's
> arrow of victory, the arrow of victory over Aram!"
> Elisha declared. "You will completely destroy the
> Arameans at Aphek."
>
> Then he said, "Take the arrows," and the king
> took them. Elisha told him, "Strike the ground."
> He struck it three times and stopped. The man of
> God was angry with him and said, "You should
> have struck the ground five or six times; then
> you would have defeated Aram and completely
> destroyed it. But now you will defeat it only three
> times" (2 Kings 13:15-19).

If the Holy Spirit hands you a weapon that does not

seem logical, use it anyway! Learn to aim and fire your supernatural weapons with skill. Be able to say with Paul, "Therefore I do not run like a man running aimlessly; I do not fight like a man beating the air" (1 Corinthians 9:26). Learning to aim and fire requires listening for the scriptures God designates for a particular need. The intercessor must learn to express those scriptures in any of the following ways.

THE NAME OF JESUS

One of the first things I learned as a growing believer was the power of Jesus' name. During my teen years, I had been involved in several seances. This activity resulted in hearing voices in the background of my mind, like a radio talk show playing at a low volume. I paid little attention to this inner radio program, occasionally tuning in to listen to some conversation. These voices were never threatening or personal, and I did not realize the source was demonic.

Only after I rededicated my life to Jesus during my first year of college did the voices change. Angry and violent, they began to torment me. I would wake up during the night with a great weight upon my body. Not able to move or speak, I could only repeat the name of Jesus in my mind. When I spoke His name mentally, I would be able to speak it aloud, and the weight and voices would vanish. It wasn't long before the "radio program" was gone for good! I have since found that this experience is not unusual.

Jesus gave us the right to use His name with all the authority that stands behind that name. It is our power-of-attorney that verifies our authority to act as His representatives:

"And these signs will accompany those who
believe: In my name they will drive out demons;
they will speak in new tongues; they will pick up
snakes with their hands; and when they drink
deadly poison, it will not hurt them at all; they will
place their hands on sick people, and they will get
well" (Mark 16:17, 18).

The prayer warrior's relationship with Jesus causes the
Enemy to tremble. The use of the name of Jesus testifies
of that relationship. Yet, we must be careful not to adopt
His name as a punctuation mark in our prayers. I often
hear others unconsciously pray, "In Jesus' name," every
time they pause to take a breath during intercession. The
key to our authority is our ongoing, intimate relationship
with Jesus, not the repetition or the volume of our
speech. Scripture relates several demonic encounters when
the name of Jesus was never mentioned, but the result
was freedom (Acts 5:15, 16; 19:11, 12). It also mentions
a demonic encounter when His name was invoked by
those who did not know Him; the result was disastrous
(Acts 19:13-17).

Our authority to act as the representative of Jesus is
also important when we operate in the role of supplicants.
A few years ago, during a family crisis, our friend Steve
was given the power-of-attorney for his father. Access to
all that was his father's became available to Steve,
because he was given the authority to act in his father's
name. He could legally represent his dad in various business situations. Often he would withdraw as much money
from his dad's bank account as necessary to conduct his
father's affairs. All he had to do was ask, in his father's

name, and the money was given him. In the same way, the name of Jesus becomes our power-of-attorney when we petition the Father as supplicants. "In that day you will no longer ask me anything. I tell you the truth, my Father will give you whatever you ask in my name" (John 16:23).

THE BLOOD OF JESUS

In chapter 8, we reviewed the victory of Calvary. It is that victory that allows us to use the blood of Jesus as a weapon. Revelation 12:11 declares, "They overcame him by the blood of the Lamb." You may have heard intercessors use the terms "claim the blood" or "plead the blood," as if the blood of Jesus was some kind of magic potion. Of course, this is not what the intercessor means! Intercessors who use these terms are applying the finished work of Calvary as a legal injunction. They are enforcing a heavenly court order against the forces of evil. Or, they may be employing the blood as the legal foundation of their petition before the Father.

As warriors, we stand in triumph, reminding evil spirits of their defeat by the Lamb's blood. As supplicants, we stand before the throne and base our appeals on the blood-bought victory of Calvary. Either might be accomplished by reciting scriptures about the blood, singing about the blood or even waving red flags symbolic of His blood. The Holy Spirit can be very creative in how we present the blood of Jesus before the throne and to the Enemy during intercession.

OUR VOICES

A person's voice plays an important role in intercession.

It can powerfully impact the unseen realm. The forces of darkness hate to hear the praises of the Lord spoken or sung, but they love to hear criticism and complaining. The Enemy seeks to silence the voice of an intercessor, because our voice exposes his defeat. Hannah prayed, "My mouth boasts over my enemies, for I delight in your deliverance" (1 Samuel 2:1). Our voices initiate spiritual weapons such as binding and loosing or speaking the name of Jesus. The following scriptures offer a variety of ways our voices can be used as spiritual warriors, supplicants and watchmen.

Proclamation. "How beautiful on the mountains are the feet of those who bring good news, who *proclaim* peace, who bring good tidings, who *proclaim* salvation, who *say* to Zion, 'Your God reigns!' Listen! Your watchmen *lift up their voices*; together they *shout* for joy" (Isaiah 52:7, 8, italics added). An intercessor often proclaims aloud that God is wanting to work in a situation. This may be spoken to the people of God or declared to the Enemy. Listen to David's proclamation as he met Goliath on the battlefield.

David said to the Philistine:

> You come against me with sword and spear and javelin, but I come against you in the name of the Lord Almighty, the God of the armies of Israel, whom you have defied. This day the Lord will hand you over to me, and I'll strike you down and cut off your head. Today I will give the carcasses of the Philistine army to the birds of the air and the beasts of the earth, and the whole world will know that there is a God in Israel. All those gathered here will know that it is not by sword or spear that the Lord

saves; for the battle is the Lord's, and he will give all of you into our hands (1 Samuel 17:45-47).

Praise. We are ordained to praise . . . to give thanks . . . to pray with understanding and in the Spirit.

From the lips of children and infants you have ordained praise because of your enemies, to silence the foe and the avenger (Psalm 8:2).

The Lord is my strength and my shield; my heart trusts in him, and I am helped. My heart leaps for joy and I will give thanks to him in song (Psalm 28:7).

So what shall I do? I will pray with my spirit, but I will also pray with my mind; I will sing with my spirit, but I will also sing with my mind (1 Corinthians 14:15).

Spoken or in song, praise will silence the enemies of the Lord. This type of praise comes from both your mind, with understanding, and from your spirit, which you may not comprehend.

Singing. Songs of praise before a battle are used by the Lord to set up ambushes against the forces of darkness:

After consulting the people, Jehoshaphat appointed men to sing to the Lord and to praise him for the splendor of his holiness as they went out at the head of the army, saying: "Give thanks to the Lord, for his love endures forever." As they began to sing and praise, the Lord set ambushes against the men of Ammon and Moab and Mount Seir

who were invading Judah, and they were defeated
(2 Chronicles 20:21, 22).

Singing is also expressed after a victory in battle as a
sign of triumph (see Exodus 15:21; Psalm 68:20-25).
During a battle, singing is a weapon used for protection
and deliverance from the Enemy: "You are my hiding
place; you will protect me from trouble and surround me
with songs of deliverance" (Psalm 32:7).

Shouting. Both Joshua and Gideon used shouting as a
spiritual weapon against their foes. Intercessors also use
shouting as a verbal recognition of the Lord's defense:
"Let all those that put their trust in thee rejoice: let them
ever shout for joy, because thou defendest them: let them
also that love thy name be joyful in thee. For thou, Lord,
wilt bless the righteous; with favour wilt thou compass
him as with a shield" (Psalm 5:11, 12, KJV).

The telling of your testimony. "They overcame him by
the blood of the Lamb and by the word of their testimony; they did not love their lives so much as to shrink from
death" (Revelation 12:11). The spoken testimony of the
saving work of Jesus Christ in your life is one of the most
powerful weapons of a warrior. This verbal recitation is
effective even if you are in your prayer closet and no one
but the Lord and demons can hear you!

Faith and confession. Faith mixed with the confession of
your mouth carries influence and acts as weapon. "I tell
you the truth, if anyone says to this mountain, 'Go, throw
yourself into the sea,' and does not doubt in his heart but
believes that what he says will happen, it will be done for
him. Therefore I tell you, whatever you ask for in prayer,

believe that you have received it, and it will be yours" (Mark 11:23, 24). Faith focuses on God's promises instead of centering on problems. By speaking in critical or fearful terms, intercessors only make the "mountain" they want removed bigger! Negative talk builds "mountains" rather than demolishing them. It defeats the purpose of intercession to criticize your mate, your boss or your pastor and then attempt to pray for them.

This does not mean we fail to see the negative in a situation. Otherwise, why would we be interceding about it! However, by speaking the truths of Scripture an intercessor is emphasizing God's power rather than continuing to rehearse the contrary works of the flesh and hell. This places us in a position to have God's heart on the circumstance and to see people through the eyes of faith: "Let us hold fast the profession of our faith without wavering; (for he is faithful that promised)" (Hebrews 10:23, KJV). Intercessors can impart either life or death, depending on what they are speaking: "The tongue has the power of life and death, and those who love it will eat its fruit" (Proverbs 18:21).

BINDING AND LOOSING

One day as Jesus was talking with His disciples, He quizzed them concerning His identity. Peter gave a simple statement that he believed Jesus to be the Son of the living God. This revelation of Christ's deity, initiated by the Father, became the foundation stone upon which the church would be built. The church became so mighty, the gates of hell were not able to withstand the force of its power. Permission for His representatives to administer Kingdom business was marked by His giving the keys of the kingdom of heaven to His church: "I will give you the keys of the kingdom of heaven; whatever you bind on earth will be bound in heaven, and whatever you loose on earth will be loosed in heaven" (Matthew 16:19).

Just as someone who is given the keys to my house has permission to freely enter and use my home, so believers have authority to conduct Kingdom business both in heaven and on earth. Keys signify this authority, while *binding* and *loosing* are ways the keys are used. Intercessors are not physically binding and loosing objects; they spiritually take authority so that things are captured or released in the spirit realm. As we pray on earth, things happen in heavenly places, which then cause circumstances to change on earth!

Sometimes new intercessors use this authority without understanding. In their zeal, they are *tying* up the things they have just *untied* through their prayers! There are times we bind the Enemy, and there are times we loose our foe's grip on situations. Often we may need to bind up the wounded or loose sickness from its attachment to someone. Note how the following scriptures refer to different aspects of binding and loosing:

- "How can anyone enter a strong man's house and carry off his possessions unless he first ties up the strong man? Then he can rob his house" (Matthew 12:29). This passage illustrates the necessity of binding a demonic spirit so that his stronghold may be ransacked.

- "And, behold, there was a woman which had a spirit of infirmity eighteen years, and was bowed together, and could in no wise lift up herself.

And when Jesus saw her, he called her to him, and said unto her, Woman, thou art loosed from thine infirmity. And he laid his hands on her: and immediately she was made straight, and glorified God" (Luke 13:11-13, KJV). The word *loosed* in this passage means to "untie or release." Sickness often needs to be untied from its connection to a person.

"I led them with cords of human kindness, with ties of love; I lifted the yoke from their neck and bent down to feed them" (Hosea 11:4). Intercessors can pray that God will embrace a person or situation with His love. He will then lead that person with cords of human kindness.

"The Spirit of the Sovereign Lord is on me, because the Lord has anointed me to preach good news to the poor. He has sent me to bind up the brokenhearted, to proclaim freedom for the captives and release from darkness for the prisoners" (Isaiah 61:1). The act of binding may serve as spiritual bandages for the wounded. Loosing happens as we declare freedom for the captives and release for spiritual prisoners.

Negative attitudes toward a person or situation will hinder our ability to use the keys of the Kingdom. Criticism leads us to place our personal judgment upon a person. This is not our place; it is God's alone. By being critical, an intercessor stands against God's purposes of restoration. Our attitudes must always be *for* the person for whom we are praying and *against* the demonic powers keeping them from God's purposes. God's heart is for people; ours should be too. Remember, we do not war against flesh and blood but against the forces of darkness. Do not bind your prayers by criticism and judgment.

Prayer warriors, supplicants and watchmen use the keys of the Kingdom as their authority to bind and loose things in the spirit realm. Warriors use these keys as they enforce Christ's victory against the forces of darkness. Supplicants use these keys as they intercede for the release of mercy and grace to broken people. Watchmen unlock the doors to their watchtowers to view the spiritual horizon. Whatever role of intercession you take, be alert to the various ways the Holy Spirit would have you use the keys of the kingdom of heaven.

Application

1. How is Scripture used as a legal library in the ministry of an intercessor? How is Scripture like a weapon's arsenal for an intercessor?

2. Give a short description of each weapon discussed in this chapter. Explain how each might also be used for supplication.

3. Describe a few of your personal experiences using some of the weapons discussed in this chapter.

4. Which of the weapons discussed might be new for you, and how might you put them to use in your times of personal intercession? . . . team intercession? . . . corporate intercession?

The Legal Library and Arsenal of an Intercessor—2

*M*ichael and Gabriel intently watched the group of intercessors. This part of their association with humans was always the most fascinating because they learned so much from their observations. They had worshiped the holiness of the Lord for eons, but the grace poured out on Calvary's cross was new to them. Although the angels had watched the plan of redemption unfold over thousands of years, they still could not comprehend the gospel of salvation (1 Peter 1:10-12; Ephesians 3:10). It was outside their realm of personal experience because they could never be one of the redeemed.

Watching supplicants who conduct research in the Lord's legal library are learning experiences for the angels. Every time they accompanied a warrior to the weapon's arsenal, they acquired a new appreciation for the grace of the Lord Jesus Christ. The highest honor was the privilege of sitting in the courtroom as a supplicant presented petitions before the Father. This was matched only by the privilege of accompanying a warrior into battle. For all of eternity future, the angels will be learning from these redeemed people because in the ages to come, the Lord plans to display them as the riches of His grace (Ephesians 2:7). For now, Michael and Gabriel attended the intercessors as they researched their supplications and inspected their weapons.

AGREEMENT

Agreement in team and corporate intercession is a mighty weapon for prayer warriors. It also secures considerable influence for supplicants as they stand before the Father. Paul stresses the importance of unity when he writes to the Philippians concerning their struggle for the spread of the gospel:

> Whether I come and see you or only hear about you in my absence, I will know that you stand firm in one spirit, contending as one man for the faith of the gospel without being frightened in any way by those who oppose you. This is a sign to them that they will be destroyed, but that you will be saved—and that by God (Philippians 1:27, 28).

The power that was released on the Day of Pentecost was preceded by believers gathering in the Upper Room "with one accord" (Acts 2:1, KJV). To be with one accord means more than just meeting for prayer; it implies a close association between those assembled. Those in one accord communicate about what they are sensing in prayer; they support each other as one unit. This association involves a mutual purpose, direction and approach to prayer assignments. Prayer participants agree on these things and then demonstrate harmony in the Spirit.

In intercession, harmony is the ability to flow together in prayer in such a way that each one praying is supporting the "music" of the others. Every person is contributing to the overall "song" of the group. A harmonious composition of prayer is created to include an intelligent agreement and ability to sense and obey the Holy Spirit as one. Disharmony is quickly spotted when someone is "out of tune" with the others or going in an independent direction.

Disunity causes us to lean toward the ways of the Enemy. Satan uses the master strategy of "divide and conquer" among intercessors. He will initiate offenses among team members, as well as disagreements over prayer assignments. Discord can be sensed even if nothing is verbalized. Satan hinders our work in the spiritual realm and causes confusion among team members. Therefore, disagreements need to be discussed and processed among the members of a team or among the leaders of corporate intercession.

Personal offenses need to be discussed privately. Differences in what people are sensing for prayer should be discussed as a team. Many times our disagreements provide important perspectives on situations and can contribute to a better understanding of the overall mind of the Lord. Other times our differences are a reflection of our prayer styles or giftings, which need to be integrated with other members of our team. Sometimes disagreement displays independence and self-focus, rather than a willingness to work together as a team. At such times, correction may be necessary.

In 1 Corinthians 1:10, Paul calls for this type of interrelationship: "I appeal to you, brothers, in the name of our Lord Jesus Christ, that all of you agree with one another so that there may be no divisions among you and that you may be perfectly united in mind and thought." Agreement acts as a weapon against our Enemy and carries authority in the courts of heaven.

One of the ways intercessors support each other is by the speaking of "Amen." This word means "So be it." Amen is spoken by someone who is in agreement with what another is praying (1 Corinthians 14:16). Verbal agreement eliminates the need for another to "re-pray" and adds more power or weight to the original prayer.

Receiving the things asked for in intercession requires that team members agree about the things they are requesting and be in harmony. Jesus joins in battle with those who pray in agreement. He stands alongside supplicants before the throne as they make their requests of the Father: "Again, I tell you that if two of you on earth agree about anything you ask for, it will be done for you by my Father in heaven. For where two or three come together in my name, there am I with them" (Matthew 18:19, 20).

FASTING

The Assemblies of God denomination is one of the strongest Christian organizations influencing the world today. Their headquarters in Springfield, Missouri, is a nurturing ground for missionaries and pastors. Few, however, realize that the midwife of this movement was an intercessor who helped birth it in the early years of the 20th century. In late 1910 or early 1911, Amanda Benedict was given a vision of storm clouds suspended over the city of Springfield. As a watchman, she viewed the approach of the Enemy, but she also knew the promises of God for this Pentecostal movement. Her response was a year of fasting and prayer. Not eating anything but bread and water for that year, Amanda stormed heaven during long vigils of intercession. Her weapon of fasting helped break the forces of evil that had threatened to abort what would become the Assemblies of God.[1]

In intercession, denying oneself a basic necessity such as food becomes a means of obtaining vital things for someone else. Fasting is a sacrifice that carries influence for supplicants as they petition the Father for the needs of others (Nehemiah 1:4—2:10). Battle plans are often revealed to intercessors as they fast (Judges 20:26-28). As a spiritual weapon, fasting brings deliverance to those bound, burdened, oppressed and yoked (Isaiah 58:6; 2 Chronicles 20:3; Esther 4:3, 16; 9:31; Matthew 17:21, KJV). In addition, watchmen will find their spiritual vision clarified as they fast for their "city" (Luke 2:36-38).

During the early days of Babylonian captivity, the prophet Daniel and his two friends were granted their request to fast. Eating only vegetables and drinking water, they became healthier than the young men who ate the royal food. King Nebuchadnezzar marveled at their knowledge and wisdom and often sought their council. He considered them 10 times wiser than all the other counselors and magicians in his kingdom. Throughout his service in Babylon, Daniel combined fasting with intercession for his Babylonian authorities and his own nation of Israel. God answered him with dreams, visions and angelic messengers. His influence before God and man was due in part to his discipline of fasting. As a result, Daniel became skilled as a supplicant, warrior and watchman.

Fasting involves more than just abstaining from some necessity of life. Proper fasting requires a right relationship with others and concern for the poor. Strife negates the purpose of fasting as does a public display of fasting (Matthew 6:16-18). The result of a legitimate fast is deliverance, revelation, guidance and restoration. The prophet Isaiah speaks of these things in one of the hallmark passages of Scripture for an intercessor. This passage ends with this promise for intercessors who fast: "Your people will rebuild the ancient ruins and will raise up the age-old foundations; you will be called Repairer of Broken Walls, Restorer of Streets with Dwellings" (58:12).

OUR HANDS

The hand of God is identified in Habakkuk 3:4 as the location of His hidden power: "His splendor was like the sunrise; rays flashed from his hand, where his power was hidden." Intercessors know that God's power is also manifest through His words or with His strong arm (Psalm 89:10; Matthew 8:16). With our hands we identify with what God is doing in the unseen realm and imitate it in the physical. Note how an intercessor's hands are used in Scripture:

🖐 "He trains my hands for battle; my arms can bend a bow of bronze" (Psalm 18:34). "Praise be to the Lord my Rock, who trains my hands for war, my fingers for battle" (144:1). God will train intercessors to use their hands and fingers in spiritual warfare. Such training will enable them to "bend a bow of bronze" in the unseen realm and against unseen enemies.

🖐 "As long as Moses held up his hands, the Israelites were winning, but whenever he lowered his hands, the Amalekites were winning. When Moses' hands grew tired, they took a stone and put it under him and he sat on it. Aaron and Hur held his hands up—one on one side, one on the other—so that his hands remained steady till sunset" (Exodus 17:11, 12). When directed by the Holy Spirit, lifted hands become a spirit weapon that brings victory.

🖐 Lifting a hand, or both hands, during intercession can bring deliverance to those cornered by the Enemy.

Tell the Israelites to move on. Raise your staff and stretch out your hand over the sea to divide the water so that the Israelites can go through the sea on dry ground. . . .' Then Moses stretched out his hand over the sea, and all that night the Lord drove the sea back with a strong east wind and turned it into dry land. The waters were divided, and the Israelites went through the sea on dry ground, with a wall of water on their right and on their left. . . .

That day the Lord saved Israel from the hands of
the Egyptians, and Israel saw the Egyptians lying
dead on the shore (Exodus 14:15, 16, 21, 22, 30).

- "Praise the Lord, all you servants of the Lord
  who minister by night in the house of the Lord.
  Lift up your hands in the sanctuary and praise
  the Lord. May the Lord, the Maker of heaven
  and earth, bless you from Zion" (Psalm 134).
  Intercessors are servants of the Lord. Many
  watchmen, supplicants and warriors use the
  night hours for their unseen ministry.
  Supplicants use lifted hands with praise as they
  petition the Lord. Warriors use lifted hands for
  many different reasons during warfare.

- "Let them praise thy great and terrible name; for
  it is holy" (Psalm 99:3, KJV). The word for *praise*
  (Hebrew, *yadah*) means "to worship with
  extended hands or graceful gestures; to show or
  point out." Hands may be used in intercession by
  extending them, gesturing or in pointing. They
  may also be used to show or act out something
  the Holy Spirit is doing in the unseen realm.

- "When he had led them out to the vicinity of
  Bethany, he lifted up his hands and blessed
  them" (Luke 24:50). Lifting the hands is used
  in invoking a blessing upon another. This is
  often part of an intercessor's assignment.

- Leviticus 7-10, 14, and 23 all mention the waving of an offering before the Lord. This was also

done during the consecration of Aaron to the priesthood (Exodus 29). Waving an offering was part of the peace offering presented when a person was thankful for something God had done. Both the trespass offering and the first-fruits' offerings were also waved before the Lord in consecration and thankfulness. In addition, the peace offering was waved in supplication as a man petitioned the Lord for mercy. Many intercessors wave their hands during supplication as an act of consecration, the expressing of thanks or a petition for someone in need.

Numbers 15, 18 and Deuteronomy 12 all refer to a "heave-offering" (KJV), an offering that is lifted up with the hands before the Lord. The heave offering was much like the wave offering and used in the same ways. This offering was also used to lift up the plunder and captives taken during war to present them before the Lord (see Numbers 31:28, 29). It was offered after taking possession of the land promised by God to the Israelites (see 15:18-21). Warriors may symbolically use their hands and arms to lift up the spoils of spiritual warfare to the Lord. In so doing, they are displaying the victory of God before the principalities and powers of the unseen realm.

"O clap your hands, all ye people; shout unto God with the voice of triumph" (Psalm 47:1, KJV). Clapping the hands is a celebration of triumph. It is used when an intercessor senses that a victory has been won. Proverbs 22:26 mentions clapping as a sign of agreement between two people. It can be used as a weapon that supports another warrior by signaling agreement in a stand against the Enemy. Supplicants will use clapping to support the petition of another team member. Many intercessors have testified to the use of clapping during times of deliverance as the powers of darkness are confronted and defeated.

"Do not offer the parts of your body to sin, as instruments of wickedness, but rather offer yourselves to God, as those who have been brought from death to life; and offer the parts of your body to him as instruments of righteousness" (Romans 6:13). The Greek word for *instruments* can be translated as "tools of war, or weapons." The Holy Spirit would have us use our hands, arms, head or any other appropriate part of our body as a weapon during intercession to bring about His righteousness. We are asked to yield them, both in righteous living and in spiritual warfare.

MUSICAL INSTRUMENTS

Musical instruments play an important part in spiritual warfare. "Every stroke the Lord lays on them with his punishing rod will be to the music of tambourines and harps, as he fights them in battle with the blows of his arm" (Isaiah 30:32). Judges 7 records the use of trumpets as one of the weapons Gideon used against the Midianites.

Miriam used dancing and instruments in proclaiming victory over Pharaoh's army (Exodus 15:20, 21). Psalm 68:20-26 describes one of the battles of the Lord with instruments as part of the triumphant procession. Musical instruments can also be a part of prophecy interwoven into intercession (1 Chronicles 25:3).

Years ago when I was in college, my roommate, Pam, and I went to the beach for some quiet time. It was late at night and Pam decided to go for a walk. I sat down by the cliff and listened to the waves breaking over the rocks below. Pulling out my flute, I began to play songs of worship and songs from my spirit. This had become a way of expressing my heart in prayer to the Lord. I often felt His presence closest during these times of musical intercession. Suddenly, there appeared a woman in front of me, walking out of the fog by the edge of the cliff. I probably jumped three feet, but I calmed down when I realized she was crying.

Sobbing, she explained that her life had no meaning and no hope. She had come to the edge of the cliff intending to jump onto the rocks below. As she contemplated her final decision she heard music floating up through the fog. Feeling compelled to follow the sound, she ended up weeping in front of me. Not knowing what else to do, I led her to the Lord! Pam arrived in time for us to answer more of her questions about Jesus, and together we took her home.

DANCING

Feet are used in spiritual warfare to stomp, march or step on the neck of a conquered spiritual enemy (Joshua

10:24; Isaiah 10:6; 25:10; Micah 1:3). Joshua used marching when he attacked the city of Jericho. In supplication,
the psalmist asks the Lord to "lift up thy feet unto the per-
petual desolations; even all that the enemy hath done
wickedly in the sanctuary" (Psalm 74:3, KJV). After a
mighty battle, David declared, "For by thee I have run
through a troop: by my God have I *leaped* over a wall" (2
Samuel 22:30, KJV). In intercession, dancing often physically portrays these actions of the unseen realm.

Part of the triumphant celebration after a victory
includes the dance (Exodus 15:20; 2 Samuel 6:14, 15). It
can also be used as an expression of joy and triumph. The
Hebrew word *guwl* means "to spin about or dance vio-
lently." This is the word for *rejoice* in Zephaniah 3:17:
"The Lord your God is with you, he is mighty to save. He
will take great delight in you, he will quiet you with his
love, he will *rejoice* over you with singing."

A supplicant often feels the spiritual travail of labor
in prayer, and the wailing of intercession can be followed by joy expressed in the dance. The Hebrew word
chuwl means "to twist or whirl in a circle" and is used
in the following passages where the words *labor* and
dancing appear: "Before she goes into *labor*, she gives
birth; before the pains come upon her, she delivers a
son. Who has ever heard of such a thing? Who has
ever seen such things? Can a country be born in a day
or a nation be brought forth in a moment? Yet no
sooner is Zion in *labor* than she gives birth to her children" (Isaiah 66:7, 8). "You turned my wailing into
dancing; you removed my sackcloth and clothed me
with joy" (Psalm 30:11).

BANNERS, STANDARDS AND FLAGS

It is the Lord's pleasure to give His intercessors banners to display before their enemies: "Thou hast given a banner to them that fear thee, that it may be displayed because of the truth" (Psalm 60:4, KJV). These banners strike fear in the hearts of the spiritual enemies of the Lord (Isaiah 5:25-27). Zechariah 9:16 identifies the people of God as His banner: "And the Lord their God shall save them in that day as the flock of his people: for they shall be as the stones of a crown, lifted up as an ensign upon his land" (KJV). It is these people, especially His intercessors, whom He lifts up against an approaching enemy: "When the enemy shall come in like a flood, the Spirit of the Lord shall lift up a standard against him" (Isaiah 59:19, KJV).

Intercessors use banners and flags as a physical connection to what the Lord is doing in the unseen realm. These banners serve several purposes. Banners are used to muster the troops for battle (Isaiah 49:22). They function as standards to which a family (intercession team) or tribe (larger church group) may rally around before setting off to battle or to regroup in the midst of battle (Numbers 1:52; 2:10). During warfare, they help direct the troops toward a place of defense and safety (Jeremiah 4:5, 6). Other times they serve to publish the news of battle and of the Lord's intentions (Jeremiah 50:2, 3; 51:27, 28). Victories are celebrated with shouts of joy and the lifting up of banners (Psalm 20:5).

Standards and banners are large flags set upon poles which can be carried before warriors in a battle. These can also be set in one place to mark the location for a unit of troops to gather. I have seen different intercession groups, each with their own standard, gather together for corporate intercession. Their standards were used not only to identify their group, but also as a sign of where they were to meet during different phases of corporate intercession. Jeremiah 51:10-12 names the watchmen as those who would set the standard upon the walls. In team and corporate intercession, the watchmen are often the ones who stand with the standards around the outer "wall," or rim of the intercessors gathered.

Flags are smaller than banners and are used for various purposes during supplication and warfare. Different colored flags represent different Scriptural truths. For example, intercessors sometimes wave blue flags to represent healing over people. Other times they will use red flags to represent the blood of Jesus. Many have testified to the spiritual breakthrough they experienced as the flags were waved over them. By listening to the Holy Spirit, intercessors will know when and how to use flags as weapons of war and in supplication.

Warriors use taffeta for individual flags of war. These snap when waved and sound like a mighty army in battle. Flags and streamers of iridescent gold, red and copper metallic material are waved to represent the fire of the Holy Spirit by supplicants as they stand before the throne. These flags can be handmade or ordered from a distributor. (Two different distributors are listed in the End Notes.)

Many teams design their own flags for intercession. Our team designed a flag with a red cross/sword (for the warrior), surrounded by the colors of gold (representing supplication), sky blue (representing the watchman), and silver (representing the heavenly realm). It serves as our church standard.

The bride of Christ is rising up as a majestic army in these last days. Her splendor is described in Song of Solomon 6:4, 10: "O my love, you are as beautiful as Tirzah, lovely as Jerusalem, awesome as an army with banners! . . . Who is she who looks forth as the morning, fair as the moon, clear as the sun, awesome as an army with banners?" (*NKJV*).

Application

1. Give a short description of each weapon discussed in this chapter. Explain how each might also be used as part of the legal library of a supplication.

2. Describe a few of your personal experiences using some of the weapons discussed in this chapter.

3. Which of the weapons discussed might be new for you, and how might you put them to use in your times of personal intercession? . . . team intercession? . . . corporate intercession?

Points of Identification for an Intercessor

*T*he "fullness of time" had finally arrived as the Son of God stepped onto the center stage of human existence (Galatians 4:4, 5). Taking on the identity of humankind, Jesus spent nine months in the womb of a woman and was born of flesh and blood. His early years were spent under the authority of His earthly parents as He attended school, did chores and eventually worked as a carpenter. He encountered the same temptations common to all, and yet He never succumbed. Jesus identified with us to the point of becoming our sin offering to pay the blood price required for those sins. His willingness to become totally identified with those He came to redeem caused anointing and authority to flow to Him from the Father (Philippians 2:5-11; Hebrews 4:14-16).

The principle of identification is also expressed in the life of an intercessor. As a supplicant, Daniel owned the sins of his ancestors in repentance so that the promises of God might be fulfilled in his day (Daniel 9). As a warrior, Joshua depended on the hands of Moses being raised in victory to secure his conquest over the Amalekites (Exodus 17:8-15). As a watchman, Isaiah was asked by God to walk naked and barefoot for three years to illustrate the barrenness of poverty and destruction that was coming upon Egypt and Ethiopia (Isaiah 20:2-4).

These odd experiences confirm the unusual aspects of certain assignments of intercession. God connects us to His heart by having us identify with those in need and with His own compassion, and by allowing us to know the Enemy's intentions. We call these connections "points of identification," because they pull us outside our normal, polite ways of prayer and place us into the deep feelings and actions of God's purposes. Sometimes our human bodies are not able to process these connections in what would be commonly considered "proper" responses.

What we experience in these times of prayer is not easily explained. Though the experience may not be attached to a scripture, chapter and verse, it is not disqualified simply because it is strange. It is only disqualified if it counters Scripture or is born of flesh rather than of the Holy Spirit. Remember, we serve a *living* God who expresses Himself in different ways. Some of these ways may appear peculiar.

Be open to God doing the unusual. Go through the Bible and write down all the reactions people had when God showed up. For example: Paul was blinded. Men and buildings shook. The priests in Solomon's temple fell to the floor. The 120 people at Pentecost acted as if they were drunk. People were delivered of demonic activity.

Ananias and Sapphira never got up off the ground. Take your pick! Intercession takes us into experiences we've never had before. As Dorothy said in *The Wizard of Oz,* "We're not in Kansas anymore, Toto."

Anointing and authority flow through the intercessor who is willing to pray from a point of identification initiated by the Lord. When coordinated by the Holy Spirit within a team of intercessors, they become a united force of awesome power. As with some of the spiritual weapons, various points of identification can be distracting in a corporate setting. Therefore, intercessors participating in a corporate gathering should take their spiritual cues from leadership as well as from the Holy Spirit, to ensure that anointing is released rather than confusion.

SINS

During the first year of the rule of King Darius, Daniel came to understand that some of the prophecies of Jeremiah and Isaiah were due to be fulfilled. Seventy years had passed since Jerusalem was desolated and Israel taken captive into Babylon. From his spiritual watchtower, Daniel knew that the promise of God's deliverance was approaching. Now was the time to intercede for the completion of the promise, that its arrival might not be hindered by the past and present sins of Israel.

The record of Daniel's intercession in Daniel 9:3-19 reveals his clear grasp of both the judgment on Israel and the promise of her deliverance. He stands in proxy for his people and "owns" the sins of his ancestors as if he had personally been involved in them. Throughout his intercession, Daniel uses the term *we* as he identifies each sin committed by Israel. This point of identification by Daniel becomes the avenue through which God ushers in the promise of freedom to a captive nation.

Intercessors may be asked by the Holy Spirit to stand in proxy for the sins of their ancestry. Atrocities committed by those before us have left gaps in the walls of our families, communities and nations. Through supplication, we can confess and repent of their sins as if they were our own. We then gain authority to stand in the gap in warfare and rebuild the walls. This does not forgive the individual sins of our ancestors, as they will still have to personally stand before the judgment seat of Christ. Yet it removes the demonic cords which may have bound us to the consequences of their sins for generations.

PHYSICAL PAIN OR WEAKNESS

Isaiah prophesied about the fall of Babylon years before Daniel deciphered the writing on the wall for King Belshazzar. As a watchman, his identification with the message caused Isaiah to feel great physical pain: "At this my body is racked with pain, pangs seize me, like those of a woman in labor; I am staggered by what I hear, I am bewildered by what I see" (Isaiah 21:3).

Intercessors sometimes say that they feel the physical symptoms of the one for whom they are interceding. Vickie often feels physical pain in different locations of her body that allow her to identify with the person for whom she is praying. Her prayers are intensified because she knows the suffering they are feeling. Although Vickie experiences these physical discomforts, there is no medical explanation for them and the symptoms disappear when she finishes her intercession.

In addition, physical symptoms cause intercessors to identify different spiritual conditions of people. A bodily illness can duplicate a spiritual illness. Heart pains allow an intercessor to know someone's internal hurt, such as the pain of divorce. The tingling or the loss of hearing in an ear might indicate the spiritual deafness of a person or group of people. Leg cramps help identify the pain of one who is crippled in their walk with God. Physical weakness is often a point of identification that allows an intercessor to fervently pray for the spiritual weakness of another.

THOUGHTS

During prayer, intercessors may have thoughts run through their minds that are not their own. This word of knowledge allows the intercessor to identify what another person is thinking. Thoughts like "I'm not worthy" or "I hate my husband" can be a point of identification. The Father's thoughts may also be heard by intercessors so that they might identify with His heart. Lustful thoughts flashing through an intercessor's mind may indicate that the person regarded in prayer is ensnared by pornography or has been sexually abused. It may also indicate the activity of a demonic spirit.

EMOTIONS

Emotions differing from the normal feelings of an intercessor could be a point of identification. Feelings of shame or uncleanness allow a person to identify with the emotional turmoil of the one for whom the intercessor is praying. Emotions may connect an intercessor to the Lord's feelings for someone in need. One weekend, Tom felt an overwhelming dryness invade his emotions when praying for a man at a retreat. The emotions were so personal and strong that Tom was devastated. Immediately he knew that this desert experience was what the gentleman was enduring in his private life. Weeping overwhelmed Tom as he felt the Father's anguish. Within a short time, the man was weeping as the Holy Spirit brought freshness and new rain to his soul.

The discerning of an evil spirit may be in the form of an identification—a personal emotion of the identity of that spirit. For example, extreme feelings of rejection, suicide or violence can come over you in the midst of intercession, indicating that you are facing these particular spirits. The feelings will not control or overpower you, but will be intense enough to catch your attention and even confuse you. You may wonder why you want to run out of the building when God has called you there to pray! The feeling of the need to escape may indicate that a demonic spirit is over-shadowing those for whom you are interceding.

WEEPING

At times weeping accompanies intense supplication. It often is the first point of identification through which the Lord calls an intercessor to prayer. An intercessor may feel an overwhelming desire to weep for no apparent reason. Sometimes this can be a sign of a chemical imbalance, much like a woman experiences as she approaches menopause. But it is often the Holy Spirit connecting the intercessor to the heart of God. The impartation of grief is God's signal that someone, somewhere, needs prayer—and soon!

The pain of others connects the intercessor with the Lord's heart of compassion. Note how the Weeping Prophet, Jeremiah, calls the people to prayer:

> The hearts of the people cry out to the Lord. O wall of the Daughter of Zion, let your tears flow like a river day and night; give yourself no relief, your eyes no rest. Arise, cry out in the night, as the watches of the night begin; pour out your heart like water in the presence of the Lord. Lift up your hands to him for the lives of your children, who faint from hunger at the head of every street (Lamentations 2:18, 19).

LABOR AND BIRTHING

Webster's dictionary defines *travail* as "painful, arduous labor; pains of childbirth; to labor with difficulty." Travail becomes a point of identification when God desires to birth something in the spirit that affects the physical realm. Paul felt this travail in his prayers for the Galatian church: "My dear children, for whom I am again in the pains of childbirth until Christ is formed in you" (Galatians 4:19). This labor process of prayer mirrors the pain and work of childbirth.

Intercessors who travail in prayer sometimes mirror the pain of childbirth. This process sometimes recurs during sessions of intercession until the plans of God are brought forth. The joy of delivery is felt when the Holy Spirit releases the intercessor from the burden.

Isaiah's prophecy for the deliverance of Israel from Babylon also became the prophecy that saw the nation of Israel birthed in 1948. In addition, this prophecy speaks to the work of intercessors in these last days. The birthing processes of God for the nations are being swiftly accomplished. It is end-time intercessors who will pray the nations into the kingdom of God:

> "Before she goes into labor, she gives birth; before the pains come upon her, she delivers a son. Who has ever heard of such a thing? Who has ever seen such things? Can a country be born in a day or a nation be brought forth in a moment? Yet no sooner is Zion in labor than she gives birth to her children. Do I bring to the moment of birth and not give delivery?" says the Lord. "Do I close up the womb when I bring to delivery?" says your God (Isaiah 66:7-9).

SYMBOLIC ACTIONS, DRAMATIZATION OR MIME

The work of intercession and prophecy is recorded by the watchman in Ezekiel 4 and 5.

> "Now, son of man, take a clay tablet, put it in front of you and draw the city of Jerusalem on it. Then lay siege to it: Erect siege works against it, build a ramp up to it, set up camps against it and put battering rams around it. Then take an iron pan, place it as an iron wall between you and the city and turn your

face toward it. It will be under siege, and you shall besiege it. This will be a sign to the house of Israel.

"Then lie on your left side and put the sin of the house of Israel upon yourself. You are to bear their sin for the number of days you lie on your side. I have assigned you the same number of days as the years of their sin. So for 390 days you will bear the sin of the house of Israel.

"After you have finished this, lie down again, this time on your right side, and bear the sin of the house of Judah. I have assigned you 40 days, a day for each year" (4:1-6).

Symbolic actions, dramatization and mime can be points of identification used between the heavenly Father and an intercessor. One day Connie and her team of intercessors walked all over the sanctuary with their eyes closed, praying for the country of China. They felt themselves walking over bridges, crossing rivers and climbing mountains. Never did they bump into the furniture in the sanctuary or stumble over things on the floor. Their verbal intercession flowed in what Connie could only identify as different dialects of Chinese.

Intercessors may sometimes mimic the cutting of scissors as cords of bondage are spiritually severed from a captive. Other times they may mime the removal of spiritual garbage by pulling these things out of a person. One church used a humorous fashion show titled *Petticoats in Combat Boots* to spiritually declare the new work God was desiring to do within their midst.

SOUNDS OF BATTLE CRIES

Certain sounds may grow in intensity within an intercessor and be released as a point of identification between the intercessor and the Lord of Hosts. Battle cries, warfare chants, and even a rhythm of sound and motion may flow from the heart of our Mighty Warrior through intercessors: "The Lord will march out like a mighty man, like a warrior he will stir up his zeal; with a *shout* he will raise the *battle cry* and will triumph over his enemies" (Isaiah 42:13). The Hebrew words *tsarach* and *ruwa* mean "whoop, roar" and a "yelling cry." Jesus is not timid about stirring up His emotions for battle. Neither should spiritual warriors be intimidated when called upon to raise a battle cry by the Captain of the Lord's Host.

WARRIOR-LIKE ACTIONS

Certain actions of warfare become points of identification. Marching, stomping, karate-type actions, whipping flags of war and wrestling an invisible enemy may seem foolish to the casual observer. Yet these actions can have meaning in the spirit realm when they are initiated by Jesus and used to identify with His warrior heart. Silently marching around the walls of Jericho for six days held no meaning for many of Joshua's soldiers. This was not their usual method of assaulting a city. Yet the spiritual significance was revealed when the walls came tumbling down.

Points of identification can be powerful tools in the hands of an intercessor. However, they must never be used apart from the Holy Spirit's directive. Intercessors who use these points to draw attention to their prayer ministry are operating from impure motives. The willingness to die to self is a key ingredient to properly being used by the Lord Jesus.

1. Why are points of identification important in the ministry of an intercessor? Do you think these are necessary to pray with power and authority? Explain your answer.

2. What are some of the points of identification that you have observed operating through other intercessors? Which points of identification has the Lord initiated in your times of personal intercession? What were the results?

3. How do these points of identification operate during team and corporate intercession?

4. How do we tell if the point of identification experienced in prayer is born of self or of the Holy Spirit?

Chapter *16* Sixteen

Strategies of an Intercessor

here is a fresh wind of the Holy Spirit blowing over intercession. Record numbers of Christians are becoming involved in praying for their churches, communities and nations. Strongholds of darkness that have existed unchallenged for centuries are being confronted and are beginning to crumble.

The basics are the same. Supplicants are gathering before the throne to pray down mercy and grace. The watchmen are reporting from their towers. Spiritual warriors continue to enforce Christ's victory against the hosts of darkness. The Scripture and armor they use will never change, but many of the strategies are new. Supplicants, warriors and watchmen are receiving new ways of presenting their petitions, expressing their prophecies and engaging in spiritual warfare. God is waking us up. Prayer is no longer dull or routine, but full of life and creative acts! God is reviving the art of intercession.

For some, the new things God is doing may seem unnecessary or even mystical. Praying over a map of a nation to intercede for the release of its spiritual captives does sound absurd. Waving flags appears as untempered zeal until a skeptic testifies to the lifting of oppression when a flag of intercession has been waved over him. The Israelites might have debated the instruction to look upon a snake held high on a pole, but their healing depended on their obedience to this obscure direction (Numbers 21:6-8). Elijah bent down to the ground and prayed for rain with his face between his knees (1 Kings 18:42, 45). Paul and Silas held a prayer meeting and worship service right after being beaten and thrown into jail. Deep pain and strong worship do not sound like a logical combination. Yet, their obedience to the Holy Spirit led to freedom and new converts (Acts 16:19-32).

SPIRIT-INITIATED STRATEGY

One of the keys to successful intercession is Spirit-initiated strategy. Knowing the Lord's objectives, having a plan on how to meet those objectives and the timing of each part of the plan are all involved. Intercession is an empty activity when initiated outside of God's direction and timing. It is one thing to perceive things in the spirit realm, but quite another thing to know what to do with what you see!

Strategy in private intercession is learned as you come to recognize the voice of the Holy Spirit. It is like wearing the bridle and reins of a horse with the Holy

Spirit as the rider. You sense His pull slowing you and directing you where to go in prayer. Each part of a prayer strategy is then guided by the Holy Spirit; all you do is listen and obey.

People often ask me for a list of scriptures they can use for a specific assignment of intercession. I usually encourage them to read through their Bible and allow the Holy Spirit to reveal the specific scriptures He wants them to use in their petitions as weapons. This advice leads to greater revelation and dependence on the Holy Spirit. They need to know the Holy Spirit as their personal strategist. They should not expect to use the same approach every time they pray.

I recently spoke at a church that had been wounded by their former leadership. After teaching, I asked those gathered to walk through the church building, praying quietly to see what they would sense in the spirit. After a while, we regrouped and each shared what they felt as they walked about the building. Our conclusions were similar. I then asked what we should do in intercession. Things that were discussed included repentance and taking dominion over several spiritual enemies who had seemingly set up camp over their church.

We formed a basic strategy for prayer. Each need mentioned was to be completely covered in prayer before moving to the next. Every person would be given the opportunity to pray about each item. At certain points, the group felt we should take specific steps in spiritual warfare and that we were to end our intercession with a song of declaration.

Once we began to pray, however, one woman stepped

in and prayed about everything. She hardly paused for breath. We had been given a strategy, but she had not listened. She was like an armored tank that plowed right through the battlefield. She did not accomplish much as her "tank" ended up in the middle of the battlefield—alone! This intercessor had neglected to switch gears from individual to team intercession. She was not accustomed to waiting on the Lord for each phase of intercession. Once teamwork was reestablished, we were able to complete the work the Holy Spirit had assigned us.

Team intercession needs to have a leader. Sometimes the leader will already have a specific strategy in mind. The team will then carry out that plan in prayer. Other times the leader will function more as an overseer who encourages each member of the team to share what they are sensing. The leader then helps the team put the "puzzle pieces" together to form the prayer strategy. Throughout the prayer time, the team may pause to share what individual members are perceiving from the Holy Spirit about the next phase of intercession. Teamwork helps confirm the direction of the Lord and allows the different giftings of the members to flow together.

Corporate intercession needs a leader, or a team of leaders, who can develop the strategy for a specific time and place of a prayer gathering. More structure is needed. The leader(s) will meet ahead of time to pray and receive information from the Holy Spirit for the corporate time of prayer. Those who attend the prayer meeting follow the instructions given by the leader(s).

When the intercession assignment is regarding breaking strongholds over churches, communities or cultures, time is needed to hear from the Lord. These strongholds are best approached by team and corporate intercessors. Usually, the Lord will first allow the team to have several encounters with the Enemy in order to learn about the opposition. Then He will begin to reveal His particular strategy for that stronghold.

It takes time to understand the demonic government that has set up a particular stronghold. Members of the team will want to know something about the forces of evil they face. Would the Lord have them approach lesser, perimeter demons before confronting the governing demonic power? Would the Lord want them to go directly to the root cause? What legal injunctions and weapons will be used and when? After revoking the right of the Enemy, what will be the approach to demolishing the stronghold? Some of God's overall strategy will be revealed during the planning stages, while other parts will be systematically revealed as the team obeys the Holy Spirit.

The siege of a stronghold that has existed for years may take months and sometimes years of warfare. The banner of truth used to revoke the right of the Enemy will need to wave throughout the team's assault. This banner is the act of repentance and/or the Scripture promises used as legal injunctions to revoke the right of the Enemy to operate his business. Anticipate the need for many different attacks to weaken the foundations of the stronghold and remove the stones of its construction. Those involved in this type of intercession should take notes of what they are learning about the opposition. They should record their actions in intercession and the results of each assault. Keeping a journal helps them clearly perceive the strategy as it unfolds. They proceed with caution and reliance on the Holy Spirit.

Intercession strategies are not always as complex as when confronting demonic strongholds. Many times intercession involves only supplication as we pray for God's grace and truth to descend on people. Sometimes healing is needed. We may be asking for the presence of the Lord to meet with His people during a worship service. Our prayers can be about leadership as we undergird them in their ministry. Strategies for these times of prayer may simply unfold during the course of intercession.

STRATEGY EXAMPLES

Reading a book, such as this one, could lead to dependence on formulas rather than on the Holy Spirit. However, it can also stretch our understanding of the numerous strategies of the Holy Spirit. We can learn from those who are experienced intercessors, and the Lord may have us use strategies already proven by successful intercession. The following examples are shared to help you understand some creative strategies I have experienced.

1. *Small groups of focused prayer.* Forming small groups is wise when many people are gathered for prayer. The larger gathering is broken into smaller units where all have an opportunity to pray. Intercessors in small groups might focus their attention on one item of prayer at a time. Objects are utilized to help those praying. This strategy of concentrated prayer is like an ongoing petition before the courts of heaven or a siege against Enemy encampments.

Group leaders are given a different object that will be used with their group. The purpose is to encourage focused prayer. Each person in a prayer group may be asked to pick a stone out of a bucket. The stones represent the people of God who are being fitted together into a spiritual house (1 Peter 2:5). Their prayer assignment is to pray as the Holy Spirit leads them about these "stones." Another group might be given a rope that is to be wrapped around the group as they pray for unity within their church. Flower seeds help another group focus their prayers on the Lord's planting process and the various "seeds" He is sowing in people's lives. A map of a town may be placed in the middle of a group as they intercede for its population.

The group prayer leader explains what the object is to represent and reminds the group to keep their prayers short. People take turns praying aloud. A requirement of speaking only one or two sentences in prayer encourages the shy person and restrains the dominant. At the end of five minutes, the leader of the prayer meeting gives a signal so each group can stop praying. Group leaders then rotate to another group with their prayer object for another five minutes of prayer. Through this manner, all groups pray about many different things in an orderly and creative fashion. Small children as well as teens and adults enjoy this procedure.

2. *Using the three roles of an intercessor.* Another strategy was used at a weekend retreat. The 60 intercessors who gathered before the Friday evening service were from many different churches and represented many different styles of intercession. They needed specific directions. They also needed a place of freedom to operate as individuals in intercession, so they could get their minds off the unfamiliar surroundings. After a short explanation of the roles of supplicants, warriors and watchmen,

the participants were handed a paper with the following information on it:

Please choose *one* of the following roles of an intercessor in which you would like to participate tonight during our preservice prayer time (normally you would probably function in all three roles, but we are short on time tonight).

Supplicants: You are not dealing with the Enemy when in supplication; you are before God's throne, facing Him and seeking Him for the needs of His people. Therefore, *come up front by the platform, find a spot to pray by yourself,* and seek the Lord, petitioning Him for the following things for this weekend:

- Pray that He will not execute judgment against those who are in rebellion to Him. Ask that God will extend mercy toward those who deserve judgment. Petition the Lord to extend His goodness that leads to repentance.

- Ask God to reveal to every person His great love and His hope for their future.

- Ask for God's grace to be extended toward participants attending this retreat, that they may receive what God has planned for them.

- Pray for the Lord's anointing to flow through the guest speaker. Ask for the Lord's peace and confidence to rest upon our guest speaker.

Watchmen on the Walls: As a watchman you are looking for two things: Enemy advancements and the promises of God. If you would like to intercede as a watchman tonight, please *place yourself along any of the walls of the room.* Watch in the spirit and intercede privately for the following things:

- Note any advancements (in the spirit realm) of the Enemy against those attending this retreat or against the purposes of God for this retreat. In the spirit, stand in the gap so these things will not enter the boundaries of this location.

- Note any of the promises of God that you sense are for this retreat and its participants. Pray that these promises arrive right on schedule and become reality in people's lives.

Warriors: As a warrior you are part of our vanguard of soldiers actively taking ground in the spirit realm. Your job is to clear the way through Enemy territory in people's lives, so that the ministry of the guest speaker will accomplish great things. If you would like to intercede as a warrior tonight, *please find someplace in the center of the room* to privately pray concerning the following needs:

- War in the Spirit so that bondages may be broken. Expect the Holy Spirit to show you specific areas of bondage that need your intercession.

- In the spirit realm, pull down any wrong reasonings or ways of thinking that you sense may hinder people from hearing what God wants to speak to them about this weekend.

Pray against anything you sense may be blocking the ministry God wants to do during this retreat.

The intercessors were then instructed to take up a position explained on the instruction paper and to intercede according to their own style of intercession. If they wanted to pray quietly, that was encouraged. If they felt they needed to speak loudly, that was also encouraged. The room was large enough for the intercessors to spread out. They were asked to focus on the prayer assignments explained in the instruction paper, as well as pray as the Holy Spirit led them.

Several key people, who were comfortable operating as supplicants, watchmen or warriors, led the way by taking up their positions. The end of the intercession time was signaled by a one-minute closing prayer by the intercession leader over the microphone. The 20-minute corporate intercession time accomplished much in prayer, and personally included all who came.

3. *A symphony of intercession.* A symphony of intercession has proven a powerful strategy when many creative intercessors are gathered together. It is reminiscent of David's bringing of the ark of God to the Tabernacle, recorded in 2 Samuel 6:12-19.

Spiritual warriors are placed around the walls of the room or an area of intercession. Some may want to war with various flags of war. They can be given specific directives for prayer or simply asked to pray for whatever the Lord reveals to them. Supplicants spread out in front and are asked to worship and appeal before the throne with specific prayer needs. Some may want to use the gold flags of worship or the fire flags, which represent the power and fire of the Lord.

Dancers are placed in areas of the room that provide enough space. Singers are placed throughout the room to intercede in song. Others are placed in the middle of the room and given streamers. They are asked to move about the room as they pray. The streamers represent the joy, celebration and freedom for which they are being asked to intercede.

The call to corporate intercession begins with the blowing of a shofar (a ram's horn) or a trumpet. Everyone then begins to intercede according to each assignment. This may sound confusing, but the end result is very powerful and moving!

The purposes and plans of the Lord can only be revealed to those who seek Him. It is out of relationship with Him that intercession strategies are birthed. Their aim is to reflect God's character, creative nature and accomplish His objectives. Knowing Jesus and learning to respond to the promptings of the Holy Spirit are the intercessor's ongoing assignment. The blessings are eternal.

Application

1. What are several strategies of intercession that you have learned from the Holy Spirit?

2. What have you found to be different between individual intercession and team intercession in following Holy Spirit-initiated strategy?

Part III

*Practical
Aspects of
Intercession*

All Intercessors Carry a Shovel

A reference from Revelation 17:3-5 is mysterious, and represents the forces of evil that will intensify their labors in the coming years.

> Then the angel carried me away in the Spirit into a desert. There I saw a woman sitting on a scarlet beast that was covered with blasphemous names and had seven heads and ten horns. The woman was dressed in purple and scarlet, and was glittering with gold, precious stones and pearls. She held a golden cup in her hand, filled with abominable things and the filth of her adulteries. This title was written on her forehead:
>
> Mystery,
> Babylon The Great,

The Mother of Prostitutes
And of the Abominations of the Earth

God requires His intercessors to walk in His holiness
and integrity. The righteousness of Jesus and the integrity of one's heart will be the marks of authority for those
who would lead His forces against end-time demonic
troops. These demons have operated on Planet Earth
since the early days of Scripture. Their demonic callings
can be identified by the corrupt character that marks
their work: pride, rebellion, rejection, violence, rage, criticism, adultery and disunity, to name a few.

An intercessor who opposes the forces of darkness
must stand free of the evil that identifies these demons.
Only humility can come against pride. Only a heart full
of God's love and acceptance toward others can counter
the spirit of rejection. Disunity is faced by those who
work for unity within the house of God. A critical spirit
is defeated by those who refuse to be critical in their own
lives. Spirits of rebellion and those of resistance to
authority are to be engaged by intercessors who move in
their relationships with a submitted heart.

God has declared that we must be holy even as He is
holy. This is a simple statement of fact, yet impossible to
perform. No one can make themselves holy before
Almighty God. Our own righteousness is as "filthy rags"
(Isaiah 64:6). Therefore, Jesus has given us His righteousness to make us holy. That is why the Cross is so
important. It is where our righteousness was forever
established. Our *position* of righteousness is no longer a
question. However, our *experience* of that righteousness is
a lifelong process. The power of the Cross must be

applied in our daily lives if we are to experience the holiness that is forever ours. The Scriptures instruct us to take some responsibility in this process as God works to conform us into His image of holiness.

This is what integrity of the heart is all about. Jesus expects us to come before Him in repentance whenever we participate in those things that He has declared are outside the boundaries of holiness. Holiness is perfected in our lives when we live in such fear of God that we refuse to continue in corruption: "Since we have these promises, dear friends, let us purify ourselves from everything that contaminates body and spirit, perfecting holiness out of reverence for God" (2 Corinthians 7:1).

It is not legalism to "purify ourselves" and to engage in "perfecting holiness." It is simply holding ourselves accountable to walk free of sin. By examining our attitudes, actions and reactions, we identify those things that grieve the heart of God. Once they are identified, we come before the Lord and allow His cleansing work to free us from their contamination. Then we will find ourselves useful for our Master and His ministries:

> In a large house there are articles not only of gold and silver, but also of wood and clay; some are for noble purposes and some for ignoble. If a man cleanses himself from the latter, he will be an instrument for noble purposes, made holy, useful to the Master and prepared to do any good work (2 Timothy 2:20, 21).

Wise intercessors maintain regular times of accountability between themselves and the Lord. Failure to do so allows the contamination of sin to leave its stench upon them when they enter into intercession for others. Demons smell this unholy odor and pay the intercessor little attention, except to encourage more contamination. The Lord also sees this contamination and grieves, because the power of His blood has not been applied to the pollution through repentance.

We all participate in sinful attitudes and actions by harboring hurt feelings, becoming defensive and being critical. Irritability crops up unexpectedly. Lust, resentment, pride and anger are embraced by a conscious choice or an unconscious habit. These are the result of living with ourselves and others who are still human! They are also things that are outside the boundary lines of God's holiness.

The Old Testament gives a vivid picture of the importance of holiness in the life of an intercessor. In Deuteronomy 23:9-14, the instructions for keeping a clean camp during warfare may be applied to those who engage in spiritual warfare:

> When you are encamped against your enemies, keep away from everything impure. If one of your men is unclean because of a nocturnal emission, he is to go outside the camp and stay there. But as evening approaches he is to wash himself, and at sunset he may return to the camp. Designate a place outside the camp where you can go to relieve yourself. As part of your equipment have something to dig with, and when you relieve yourself, dig a hole and cover up your excrement. For the Lord your God moves about in your camp to protect you and to deliver your enemies to you. Your

camp must be holy, so that he will not see among
you anything indecent and turn away from you.

The camp of an intercessor is where one resides
between battles. It is also where the prayer warrior meets
with those on a prayer team or those comprising corporate intercession. Lack of a clean camp invites "flies" and
other disease-carrying, spirit-type insects into the area of
intercession. This spiritual camp must be kept clean. The
presence of the Lord depends on it.

The uncleanness mentioned in Deuteronomy 23 is
everyday sin that results from being human. Irritation,
defensiveness, and lust for a beautiful person are examples. These sins do not cause contamination if repentance is immediate. But if we participate for any length of
time in these sins, they cause defilement to ourselves and
others. Sexual dreams that become a daytime fantasy are
an example. Irritation that becomes anger and erupts on
others is another.

Prayer warriors who find themselves contaminated by
such sins should leave the camp and find cleansing
before the Lord. In other words, excuse yourself from
intercession and deal with your own contamination. This
may take time, especially if others have been exposed to
your sin and need to hear an apology. Be prepared to step
out of intercession, particularly team or corporate intercession, for a few hours.

One of the things included in a warrior's weapons in
ancient times was a small digging tool or shovel. This
was to be used when visiting the designated area of the
"bathroom" outside the camp. Intercessors also carry a
"shovel." It is called the shovel of repentance and is used

whenever we need to visit the designated place for spiritual excrement. This place is outside the camp of intercession, yet within the privacy of our own prayer dealings with the Lord.

This is significant for prayer warriors who intercede alone. It ensures a clean place in the spirit realm where intercession for others is begun. This principle of cleanness is vital in team intercession, for each person contributes to the cleanliness of the camp. I have met intercessors who believe it their right to relieve themselves of critical thoughts and anger in the midst of team intercession. The result has been confusion and contamination among other team members.

The Lord walks about the camp of intercession to bring protection and victory. If He sees anything indecent, He turns away. All intercessors must carry their shovel of repentance and use it! God's requirement of holiness in Deuteronomy 23 is serious: "For the Lord your God moves about in your camp to protect you and to deliver your enemies to you. Your camp must be holy, so that he will not see among you anything indecent and turn away from you" (v. 14). This is the holiness referred to in Job 22:30 that brings answers to prayer: "He will deliver even one who is not innocent, who will be delivered through the cleanness of your hands."

Our ability to be used by God in spiritual warfare is directly related to our personal obedience:

> For though we walk in the flesh, we do not war
> after the flesh: (for the weapons of our warfare are
> not carnal, but mighty through God to the pulling
> down of strong holds;) casting down imaginations,

and every high thing that exalteth itself against the
knowledge of God, and bringing into captivity
every thought to the obedience of Christ; *and having in a readiness to revenge all disobedience, when
your obedience is fulfilled* (2 Corinthians 10:3-6,
KJV, italics added).

Our holiness has already been secured by Christ Jesus.
However, the experience of that holiness is dependent
on our obedience. It is the motives and attitudes of the
heart that constitute a holy life. Let's look at five of the
many attitudes and motives the Lord wants us to dispose
of outside the camp.

1. *An attitude of resistance.* We do not mean to be
resistant to others. We are only concerned and state our
anxiety in a wrong manner. Usually we will receive a
negative reaction from a person in authority, who senses
resistance rather than concern. Husbands and wives are
a good example of those who feel resistance when their
mate is expressing their anxiety inappropriately. Parents
misinterpret their teen's opinions when it is just the
teen's immature way of communicating fears or concerns. Pastors react to those who share their concerns as
"thus says the Lord." Proper communication is a key to
walking free of rebellion or the appearance of resistance.

When we consciously or unconsciously walk in resistance to authority, we contaminate the camp and allow
entrance for demonic activity. These demons follow us
into intercession and cause roadblocks. (Resistance
leads to resistance!) Resistance to authority may be spoken or unspoken.

Some intercessors try to live independent of spiritual

oversight to avoid accountability to those God has set in His church to pastor His people. Others act "spiritual" and mark any authority (such as a pastor or other leader) as a controller or one who has a "Jezebel spirit" (Jezebel was a queen who used manipulation and control as marks of her authority). They then use prayer as a subtle way to manipulate situations and people. Repentance is needed when we have resisted the authorities God has placed in our life; it is also vital when we have improperly communicated our concerns.

2. *False intimacy*. Intercession is a high calling, requiring intimacy. Everything that we are and do stems from our intimacy with God. It is He who has created us for intimacy with Himself; He even calls us His bride. Intercession focuses on that intimacy, because we are people who plead for others in the closeness and security of the Father's love. We must walk in an attitude of worship, joy and holiness. Intimacy with Jesus must be the ongoing experience of every intercessor.

Our wholesome relationship with our mate reflects the security and joy of intimacy with God. The intimate relationship between a man and his wife was intended by God to be untainted by others, even in the mind. Television sitcoms and romantic novels can be dangerous when they lead us into sexual imaginations. These fantasies are called false intimacy, because they are outside the mental boundary lines of holiness. Entertaining any type of false intimacy is a form of adultery. It also is spiritual adultery, because it defiles our relationship with our holy God.

Pornography, sexual fantasies or anything counterfeiting true intimacy will hinder true intercession. Many of the end-time battles will be with spirits of sexual sin.

Intercessors must be prepared. The shovel of repentance is needed to bury false intimacy outside the camp of intercession.

3. *Criticism.* Criticism is more than words; it is the expression of our heart. We all have times of frustration with others; that is just a part of life. It is what we choose to do with our frustration that gives us influence with God and people and qualifies us to be agents of change in any situation. A negative and critical attitude indicates that we are not processing our frustration "outside the camp." We sound more like the "accuser of the brethren" rather than a representative of Jesus!

How can we pray for others if we have one foot in the camp of the Enemy? To criticize another person is evidence that we do not have the basic revelation of wrestling against principalities rather than flesh and blood. We must take our frustrations and process them alone with Jesus. Then we will be qualified to intercede in the power of His grace.

4. *Offense.* Hurt feelings, anger and other reactions of offense signify that something is in our heart that needs to be corrected. Pride, unteachableness or self-pity could be the culprits. By examining ourselves, we can repent of these defiling sins before they affect others. Self-examination also provides an opportunity to seek God's grace when we are on the receiving end of another's immature and hurtful behavior. It gives us an opportunity to practice being ambassadors of grace.

5. *Pride.* Most of the intercessors I know are those who walk humbly. They walk *among* other intercessors rather than *over* them. They are continual learners who respect the spiritual weight of those with whom they learn. This

attitude qualifies many for leadership. Yet, I am always surprised to encounter those who think they are "God's gift of intercession" to a group of people. Some intercessors stop learning from others and become "the all-wise one." They always know the "inside story" of what is going on in the spirit realm, and they express it in ways that display their "spirituality." Often, they disassociate themselves from a church and operate independently. They believe that no pastor or church in town has the inside "scoop" on spiritual things as much as they.

Another form of pride is just as dangerous. It is called inferiority and focuses on "self." Focusing on our own deficiencies is a lack of faith. It distorts what we hear from the Lord and causes confusion. Confidence is built when we get our focus on the Lord and those around us.

Brought into team intercession, inferiority hinders the team by causing others to be overly sensitive. Team intercession requires that we lay aside our inadequacies and intermingle our spiritual giftings with others. We become a powerful unit when we understand that the flow of the Spirit of God is dependent on our gift as much as the gifts of the other members of the team. The whole team is hindered if attitudes of inferiority keep us from contributing our portion.

It does not take much time to check our heart. If there are unholy things within our heart, we can bury them before we ever enter the camp of intercession. Some teams have a "heart check" before they begin prayer by asking each other if they have repented of all their "stuff" before coming to intercession. A simple answer of "yes" is all that is needed. The team members know that an answer of "no" requires that the person remove himself for the time being. That team member would need to find a quiet place to be alone with Jesus. He then is free to reenter the camp and participate in intercession. Teams who understand the importance of a clean camp will find that the Lord walks among them to protect them and deliver their spiritual enemies into their hands.

Application

1. Why is it important for an intercessor to understand the difference between positional and experiential holiness?

2. What evidence have you seen that would indicate the lack of a clean camp in your own times of private or team intercession?

3. What might be some heart attitudes and motives that you must hold yourself accountable to bury outside your camp of intercession?

Avoiding the Pitfalls of Intercession

*V*icki was confused. Jenny (a pseudonym) had indicated a desperate need to meet with her for prayer. Her humble attitude and desire for a prayer partner had touched Vicki's merciful heart. Yet each time they met, Vicki found that Jenny had already decided the Lord's will about her need and chose the focus of their praying. In reality, Jenny was consuming Vicki's time and asserting herself as a spiritual mentor. The prayer sessions were exhausting Vicki, emotionally and spiritually.

Vicki had fallen into one of the pitfalls of intercession. Her innocent and caring heart connected her to someone who was not what she appeared. Vicki began to research Jenny's background and found that her "humility" was actually a false covering for resisting authority. Moreover, a reputation of being unteachable was the legacy Jenny had left behind in the many churches she had previously attended. The wisest move for Vicki was to cut herself off from this religious spirit. By doing so, Vicki was released from confusion and exhaustion.

Pitfalls are hidden holes or snares laid along a pathway. They hinder those walking on the path and, in many cases, prevent these individuals from continuing their journey. Pitfalls are avoidable if we know what they look like and maintain our vigilance. The Enemy uses them to entrap an intercessor. Lack of wisdom and prudence can cause even the innocent to fall. Wise intercessors learn from their mistakes and erect "Danger— Don't Go Here" signs next to known pitfalls.

Those who are pure in heart can end up in a hidden pitfall simply because of their lack of experience or understanding. They may have failed to count the cost of intercession or forgotten to take a needed pause from their ministry of prayer. Other times, they may trip into certain pitfalls characteristic to the different roles of intercession. Each role of a supplicant, warrior and watchman has certain danger areas that can entrap the innocent. Advanced warning can safeguard even the inexperienced.

THE SUPPLICANT'S BURDEN

Supplicants frequently feel such intensity of prayer that it becomes an all-consuming burden within them. They walk into the grocery store feeling depressed. Having coffee with a friend is dull, because of the heaviness they are still carrying. Their depression will follow them into a time of worship. They may even feel an intense feeling of grief.

It takes awhile for supplicants to understand that these consuming feelings are not about themselves. The weight they feel is the call of the Holy Spirit to intercede about something they may or may not know. It is one of those points of identification discussed in an earlier chapter. However, to experience a point of identification in prayer is one thing; to own it outside the prayer closet causes confusion and discomfort to those around you. Most people will not be able to identify with what you are feeling. Their callings are in different areas. It takes discipline to separate the burden of prayer from one's life among other people.

Once intercessors know the burden is not about themselves, they may still be confused as to what to do with this enormous weight. Finding a secluded place to travail in prayer is the first avenue to releasing the burden. Some churches provide a prayer room to which their intercessors can retreat. The privacy of such a place allows for loud weeping and wailing or other forms of intense intercession. The rest of the congregation is undisturbed, yet important business of the Spirit can still be conducted.

If a place of prayer cannot be found in our homes, churches or other locations, the burden must be set aside until we can find one. If we are participating in a team or corporate setting, we must put the burden "on hold" until we sense the timing of the Holy Spirit for the release of travail. Setting aside a burden of prayer or putting it "on hold" is not unspiritual. Rather it is very spiritual. We are reminded in 1 Corinthians 14:32, 33 that "the spirits of prophets are subject to the control of prophets. For God is not a God of disorder but of peace." Learning self-control avoids pitfalls.

THE MILITANT HEART OF A WARRIOR

Those who have the warrior's heart tend to view every prayer assignment as an opportunity for demonic confrontation. They just love beating up the Enemy! This excitement, however, can cause intercessors to foolishly rush in where wise men fear to tread. Spiritual warfare is no game. A few easy victories can cause overconfidence, until they find themselves lying flat on their backs in the pitfall of presumption.

For a prayer warrior, waiting on orders from the Commander in Chief, Jesus, is often difficult. Jesus seldom does things the same way twice. He tends to vary His battle plans. This throws the forces of evil into confusion, for they never know what the Lord is going to do! Learning to patiently listen for the Lord's battle plan keeps a warrior from presumption. The weapons issued, the timing of confrontation, and the manner in which the confrontation and weapons are used will vary. Dependency on the Lord is the key to every step the warrior takes in spiritual warfare.

Not everything that is prayed for should come from a warrior's viewpoint. Works of the flesh need grace, mercy and correction released from the throne of God, not demonic confrontation. Prayer assignments that involve grief and loneliness call for the comfort of the Holy Spirit. This may be difficult for warriors to understand, as they tend to see demons behind every problem! Sometimes a militant perspective can cause a warrior to unintentionally dominate a prayer team or corporate intercession. Recognizing that supplication is also part of intercession will give balance to those who are overzealous. It will also stretch their experience.

A "Watchman on the Walls" or an "Elder at the Gates"

Intercessors serve a vital role in the life of a local church. They war in secret for things that threaten individuals or their corporate fellowship. Their work can be intense, unseen, unacknowledged and lonely. They understand what it means to "stand in the gap." However, it is often in the additional role of "watchman" where an intercessor will encounter frustration.

Earlier we discussed the role of watchmen. Their duty is to watch for danger and alert the city when needed. But an intercessor needs to be aware of other positions within the city, because they will often work closely with the people in those positions. Within the city, near the temple, are the worship leaders, whose main duty is to prepare and lead the city in worship. Service people scurry about doing the many duties that keep a city running smoothly. Teachers are busy with educating folks, and medical teams minister to those deeply wounded.

Sitting in the dust at the city gates are the elders of the city. A lot happens at the city gates, because a lot of traffic passes in and out the entrance within view of the elders. That is where they meet to discuss issues and make legal decisions. City expansion and councils of war take place as those elders sit in the dirt. Above all this, the intercessor stands in his watchtower and scans the horizon for any sign of danger, always ready to give a cry of warning.

Intercessors face frustration when the "city" doesn't respond to their cries of warning. They often feel a sense of responsibility for the danger coming, and they panic when others don't seem to see it. They meet with the elders at the gates, but at times the elders don't recognize the peril. When the intercessors perceive that the leadership isn't heeding their warnings, they begin to believe that blood will be required at *their* hands, because they discern the danger (Ezekiel 3:16-19). In desperation, some intercessors may usurp authority. They end up causing confusion, discord and appear rebellious. Other times they just fume within their watchtower and contemplate finding a new job in a new city.

It is the role of a watchman to alert the elders about things approaching the city. Many times, the elders are unable to focus on the danger until it gets closer. What may appear imminent and urgent to a watchman on the wall appears distant and unimportant to an elder at the gates. There have been things that intercessors have seen afar off and brought to the elders' attention, only to find that they took 10 years to come to pass! That didn't mean that the intercessors were wrong; just that things that seem to be close in the telescope of an intercessor are often more distant than they appear!

The responsibility of the watchmen is to leave the decisions concerning that danger in the hands of the leaders. Watchmen are not responsible for the government of the city. What happens to that information after it is submitted to the leadership is not their burden; accountability before the Lord has passed from the watchmen to the elders at the gates. Furthermore, there are no guarantees that leadership will wisely process the information an intercessor submits. The watchmen should continue to intercede concerning the information, but they will not have to answer to the Lord concerning its outcome.

It helps to remember that the elders at the gates are receiving information from other watchmen positioned on other parts of the city walls. Their vantage points offer different perspectives for the elders to consider. The account of one watchman must be weighed by what another is reporting. For example, if the northern watchman sees danger approaching from the north, the southern watchman may have spotted reinforcements arriving from the south. Reports from nearby cities, and problems within their own walls are also under consideration. The elders must take all this into account, along with what they are hearing directly from the Lord concerning timing, direction and strategy. This is no easy task! An intercessor who understands his place as a watchman and continues to intercede for leadership, without assuming the responsibilities of the elders at the gates, will walk free of certain pitfalls.

THE COST OF INTERCESSION

No war is ever sporting; spiritual warfare is no exception. Throughout history individuals have put their lives in jeopardy to save their families. Many fought on foreign battlefields, others on their own soil. All were willing to lay down their lives to serve their country. Countless were killed. Some were wounded. Others were captured by enemy forces and later delivered. A few were declared missing in action. All formed bonds with their comrades that remained the rest of their lives. So it is with soldiers of intercession.

Most Christians are willing to become warriors in these spiritual battles once they have encountered the evils that threaten to invade their homes and churches. There are risks and people can get hurt, but that does not mean we do not become involved. George Otis Jr., in his book *The Last of the Giants*, says, "It is a salient fact of spiritual engagement that God almost never calls His people to a fair fight. The recurring theme of Scripture is one of giants and multitudes. Time and again Christian warriors were asked to face foes whose natural resources exceeded their own."[1]

Considering the cost of personal involvement is part of the preparation for battle. In so doing we can avoid many of the pitfalls common to intercession. In Luke 14:28-32, Jesus gives the following instructions to His disciples:

> "Suppose one of you wants to build a tower. Will he not first sit down and estimate the cost to see if he has enough money to complete it? For if he lays the foundation and is not able to finish it, everyone who sees it will ridicule him, saying, 'This fellow began to build and was not able to finish.' Or suppose a king is about to go to war against another king. Will he not first sit down and consider whether he is able with ten thousand men to oppose the one coming against him with twenty thousand? If he is not able, he will send a delegation while the other is still a long way off and will ask for terms of peace."

The time required to be involved in intercession needs to be considered. Also, weigh your level of understanding of intercession and find someone as a mentor if necessary. A prayer team can often meet this need as they progress together into the things of the Spirit. Furthermore, expect God to put you through some basic training in the Holy

Spirit's "boot camp"! The cost of learning is ongoing—continue to listen, ask questions, read, attend seminars and grow in your calling!

An intercessor can expect to meet occasional misunderstanding and ridicule from believers and unbelievers alike. Truth may be twisted and misrepresented by others. At the most inconvenient time, sickness can approach a prayer warrior. Irritability and confusion may seem to settle over the family, or a series of weird demonic encounters may suddenly occur. Satan will stir up trouble in many different forms in hopes of waylaying an intercessor. Sometimes they may experience a backlash of such events during and after a significant period of intercession. This is part of the cost one must consider (Ephesians 6:13).

In many areas of the world, Christians are being persecuted and killed for their faith. Intercessors are no exception. We can expect this to increase in the end times, as the Book of Revelation describes the future as a time of persecution and suffering. The only comment Revelation makes toward those being martyred is to call "for patient endurance and faithfulness on the part of the saints" (Revelation 13:10; 14:12). What an understatement! Yet it speaks volumes. It indicates that these end-time saints have foreseen persecution. They understand Calvary and their mission of making the name of Jesus known. Their patience and faithfulness have already been forged in the trials of life. Now they are ready to face the trials of death.

Count the cost. Learn now what it means to war in the Spirit so that later it will be second nature. Consider carefully Jeremiah 12:5: "If you have raced with men on foot and they have worn you out, how can you compete with horses? If you stumble in safe country, how will you manage in the thickets by the Jordan?"

EXEMPTIONS FROM WARFARE

Scripture indicates some should refrain from warfare for a variety of reasons. In the Old Testament, certain warriors were assigned to guard the supplies at the base camp, while others went off to war (1 Samuel 25:13; 30:24). Deuteronomy 20:5-7 speaks of those who have just built a house, planted a vineyard or become engaged to marry as needing to refrain from battle so that they might enjoy these new blessings that God has given. Verse 8 states, "Is any man afraid or fainthearted? Let him go home so that his brothers will not become disheartened too." In Judges 7:1-8, the Lord required Gideon to reduce his army from 32,000 men to 300 in one day! God doesn't require numbers as much as He requires courage and alertness. A person who is experiencing fear or discouragement can spread these attitudes to others.

It would seem there are times when one should refrain from participating in intercession. Sometimes an intercessor needs to take some R & R (rest and relaxation) alone with the Lord. It is not that this person neglects prayer. Rather, the focus is on personal enjoyment and fellowship with Jesus rather than on the needs of others.

Our relationship with the Lord is defined in more ways than just our role as an intercessor. An intercessor is also a worshiper, disciple, servant and friend of Jesus. There is coming a time when an intercessor's role as warrior will diminish, for the battles will be no more. Jesus is more than just our Mighty Warrior; He is also our King, our Shepherd, our Prince of Peace and our Bridegroom.

Application

1. Describe some of the pitfalls you have encountered as a supplicant, warrior and watchman. In what ways are you able to relate to the pitfalls described in this chapter?

2. What must you consider as part of the personal cost of intercession? What price have you paid to be an intercessor?

3. What are some Scriptural reasons for not participating in the ministry of intercession? How do you know when you must take time out for R & R?

Chapter **19** *Nineteen*

Pastor to Pastor

Pastor Steve Witmer served as senior pastor of Wellspring Christian Church in Dinuba, California, for many years. He currently serves as the unit superintendent of Northwestern Canada for the Foursquare denomination. Highly respected as a "pastor's pastor," I asked Steve to write concerning his observations in pastoring intercessors. The following letter was his response:

Dear Sue,

Thank you for the opportunity to pen a few lines regarding how to relate and work with intercessors. I have questioned many times my suitability to address this arena, since I am on a major learning curve myself. However, laying these insecurities aside, here are a few thoughts that I believe pastors should consider.

Pastors have a unique role and responsibility in leading and working with intercessors. There has never been a period in history where intercession is more necessary and more misunderstood. It is like an ancient tool, too long neglected, but only now rediscovered by individuals and restored through the agency of the Holy Spirit. What follows, therefore, is not a complete assessment of intercession. It is rather a few hints I am learning to implement for the releasing and affirmation of this essential ministry tool in the life of our assembly.

Much of what I have learned has to do with myself! Any new release of the Spirit, through the use of a gift given to people, requires that I be stretched beyond my current comfort zone. A hundred questions flood my mind, while a dozen fears invade my soul. I am learning to trust God in new ways, since He is the Lord of the church, and the gifts He dispenses are all good gifts. To relax and allow God to move as He will through these intercessors, in the way He chooses, is likely the greatest lesson of all.

What really is meant by "decently and in order"? Times of God's great intervention in the affairs of humanity, called revival, have always included activities that would have been considered inappropriate in quieter seasons. This is true also of the release of power-filled intercession. As a pastor who tends to observe this phenomenon from a subjective distance, I am regularly beyond my comfort zone. Yet the fruit of intercession has clearly proven that the activity or demonstrative action was God-breathed.

Have you ever wondered why Jesus spit and made a mud poultice to apply to the blind man's eyes? After much contemplation, I have come to the conclusion that "God's ways are not my ways . . ." and that the true and ultimately deeper issue is, "Who is really in control, God or me?" To harness intercessors and retain the reins is a folly that will ultimately drive the carriage off the cliff. Do yourself a great favor and let God drive intercession and the intercessors in the direction of His highest purposes.

Having stated the above, allow me to strike a posture of balance in leading intercessors. A pastor must not back away from leading these gifted individuals. With full appreciation for the differing ministry gifts and functions, we must both release these into their role, while fulfilling the part God has given us to play in the life of the church. Pastors are shepherds; they are responsible to care for a flock. Exercise your leadership gift to gently lead intercessors to greater growth—personally and spiritually. God has ordained that intercessors are sheep too! They need the protection their local shepherd provides. His wisdom is essential; his discernment is crucial; his ability to see the big picture provides stability, and his gentle love and correction provides the safety necessary to make mistakes and learn by them. In summary, intercessors intercede while pastors pastor so that the whole church will benefit.

Let us shift for a moment to the pastor's role in the mechanics of intercession. It has been my discovery that seldom does the Spirit endorse my preplanned list or prayer agenda! Prepackaged programs with predetermined topics tend to fly like lead balloons with true intercessors. Intercession, after all, is a function of the Holy Spirit as He moves our heart on behalf of another. Waiting on God's direction is frequently difficult for me. Too often I conclude that my list of critical issues must be the primary direction of the Spirit for the meeting. My impatience often dilutes the power of prayer by "watering down" God's plan for that session.

Be willing to wait and ascertain the direction of the "wind of intercession." Often the intercessory group will be more "in tune" than you. Stand in your place of covering and protection and discern the direction of the intercession. Are the intercessors perceiving Satan's scheme and plans? Join them in praying with authority to foil Satan's attempts. Are the intercessors tapping into God's desires and intentions for someone or something? Agree with them in prayer for "God's will to be done on earth." Are the intercessors responding to the Spirit of God for the needs of another? Stand in the gap with them for rescue and release. Often your discernment and perspective can aid the intercessors in being more effective in praying what they are sensing in the Spirit.

Lastly, what about those problematic few who use intercession to gain a platform to showcase their spirituality? Be careful not to "throw the baby out with the bath water" by shutting down Spirit-led intercession because it gets messy at times. The principle that comes into play is this: The immature will occasionally do things that demonstrate their immaturity. Scripture encourages us not to execute them by killing their zeal. Rather, we are to exhort them by challenging them to grow into a more selfless use of the gift. As difficult as it is to divide between soul and spirit, the prize of a fully released, safe and mature intercessor is a valuable asset in the life of any assembly.

There is a simple caution that needs to be expressed at this point: Not all intercessors will look and minister the same way. God is delighted with variety and godly individuality. Guard against the more militant and aggressive becoming the standard for the group, so that perhaps the reflective "weepers" feel less gifted or unspiritual. Strive to welcome all expressions of the flow of the intercessory gift. Toss out the cookie-cutter mold. God does not have any in His heavenly tool chest!

In conclusion, it is helpful to remember that we are all on a constant and fairly steep learning curve. As God releases more intercessors to greater levels of intercession, there will be more emphasis and stress placed on character. It will become less important what we do and increasingly essential who we are and what we are becoming in Christ. Give room for the defining and refining work of the Spirit in the lives of intercessors. God is very skilled at "finishing the good work" He has begun in them.

May God grant you great grace, persevering patience and hopeful expectation as together we believe for the lost art of intercession to be released on the church. May the Great Shepherd lead each of us "under-shepherds" into the green pastures of provision and the still waters of renewal in these days.

Blessings in Jesus,
Pastor Steve Witmer

Notes

CHAPTER 7

[1] *The Ultimate Weapon*, by Francis Frangipane, July 1995 cassette tape by Morningstar Publications

CHAPTER 14

[1] Taken from an article by Joyce Wells Booze, "Amanda Benedict Prayed," *Pentecostal Evangel*, Feb. 15, 1996.

[2] Distributors for flags:

- West Coast Pageantry, PO Box 18482, Irvine, CA 92623-8482
- Freedom Flags, Instruments of Worship, Ronda Robb, 1250 San Ramon, Atascedero, CA 93422.

CHAPTER 18

[1] George Otis, Jr. *The Last of the Giants* (Grand Rapids: Chosen Books, 1991), 263.